IT'S MY WORLD TOO

Accepting Challenges, Embracing Life

HOMER L. PAGE

abbott press®
A DIVISION OF WRITER'S DIGEST

Abbott Press books may be ordered through booksellers or by contacting:

Abbott Press
1663 Liberty Drive
Bloomington, IN 47403
www.abbottpress.com
Phone: 1-866-697-5310

Because of the dynamic nature of the Internet, any web addresses or links contained in
this book may have changed since publication and may no longer be valid. The views
expressed in this work are solely those of the author and do not necessarily reflect the
views of the publisher, and the publisher hereby disclaims any responsibility for them.

Any people depicted in stock imagery provided by Thinkstock are models,
and such images are being used for illustrative purposes only.
Certain stock imagery © Thinkstock.

ISBN: 978-1-4582-1418-8 (sc)
ISBN: 978-1-4582-1419-5 (hc)
ISBN: 978-1-4582-1420-1 (e)

Library of Congress Control Number: 2014902264

Printed in the United States of America.

Abbott Press rev. date: 02/19/2014

To Angie, my wife, my friend, my partner
in the best decades of my life

CONTENTS

CHAPTER 1

Why Does It Matter?

I HAVE WRITTEN A BOOK in which I am the central character. Since I am not a celebrity nor a great athlete nor a famous politician, an explanation is in order. Why does my story matter? Why should a reader want to know about my life? I offer my answer with humility.

I have lived my life with purpose. I am a blind man who refused to accept a passive role, even though there were many times when others urged that path upon me. Each of us struggles to make our way in life, to establish families, to find meaningful work, and to connect with our community. We think those who succeed in this struggle are successful, happy people. It is not always easy to achieve this level of success; however, the courage to make the effort and the determination to not quit in the face of social barriers and personal failures are necessary qualities if we are to achieve a good and useful life. In our time there are many stories of lives gone astray, talents wasted, opportunities squandered; however, this is not my story. I have struggled to build a good and useful life, and I have succeeded. I hope the reader will agree that the struggle to live successfully still matters.

In the pages that follow, I tell my story. My account is personal and, at times, close to the bone. However, I sincerely believe we share a common humanity, and the more true and personal my story is, the more it resonates with others. I am blind. Most of my readers will not be; yet my challenges are not so different from those faced by others. I have worked to cast off the misplaced culturally imposed limitations, as have many others. I have searched for those experiences and opportunities that have allowed me to build a positive self-identity. As many others, I have succeeded and failed, experienced joy and despair, and learned to affirm myself in a challenging and ever-changing world. I have struggled to find the courage to act and the wisdom to accept what I cannot change.

My blindness creates one of the conditions that shapes my life. It limits and challenges me. However, everyone has conditions that shape his or her life and must be accepted and accommodated. It is this common humanity that I address. If I tell my story truly and well, I believe every reader can find a link. This is my purpose in writing this book. As we tell our stories, the listener realizes that what might have at one time sounded foreign is, in fact, quite recognizable. The last half century has been a trying time in the history of our nation. We need to share our experiences of living and trying to understand our world. Many forces pull us apart, but there is much that holds us together. If we talk about our lives, I believe we can define a common bond.

Over the years I have spoken many times to groups about blindness. My listeners often ask, "What is it like to be blind?" This is a complex question to answer. There are attempts to simulate the experience. Individuals will wear blindfolds. Restaurants will serve food in total darkness. Children will close their eyes, but the total experience is more than not seeing. Blindness encompasses age-old stereotypes, social expectations concerning the capacity of blind persons, and some genuine physical limitations. It requires accommodations to the technology of the age, and above all, it challenges the blind person to carve out a life and a personal identity that one can affirm for a lifetime. This is my attempt to share with the reader the complex reality that is blindness and the way in which I have responded to it. In the end, I believe the reader will discover my experiences and strategies are not so different from his or her own.

The story that I tell in this book is largely one of a happy life. I am blind, and I have been blind since birth. I have engaged in my world and the events that have made its history in my time. I grew up in a strong family, received an excellent education, had a successful and challenging career, and achieved a satisfying personal life. Life is good for me, but as in the lives of all people, I have faced my own challenges. It is in the context of living in the world as a blind person that my story unfolds, and it is as a blind person that I have claimed my place.

Throughout my life I have often been told, "You can't." My answer has been, "Yes, I can." I and many other blind and disabled persons have faced the doubt and skepticism of others as we have tried to make our way in the world. Often the negativity of others is inspired by the best of intentions. They fear for our safety, seek to protect us from the disappointment associated with what they believe to be certain failure, or simply are concerned that our efforts are absurd. I have learned and accepted my limitations, but no one has the right to set those boundaries for me. Only I can define my limits. The challenge of every person with a disability is to be strong enough to reject the condescension and destructive negativity of others, while remaining open to their genuine goodwill. This is not always easy to do, but it is not pleasant or productive to live in a constant state of anger. I have steered as best I can through the rocks presented by this challenge. I hope my story can be helpful as others try to travel the same course.

It's My World Too is the title of this book, and it is also the title of a planned series. I have chosen this title because it states a claim. Often persons with disabilities are forced to sit on the sidelines of life, while others get into the game. My title proclaims that I refuse to be a spectator while others play. I am claiming the world for myself. It is my world too. This book is my story of how I have gone about making good that claim. I will tell the stories of others in subsequent publications. I believe these stories provide important testimony to the strength of the human desire to be a part of the inclusive human community, and they provide proof that our social order has come a long way toward fulfilling the promise that was first made in the Declaration of Independence. Each of us has the right to equality, liberty, and the pursuit of happiness. Our stories tell how we have taken possession of that fundamental right.

Declaring a right and making the claim stick are two very different things. If one is a person with a disability, one must deal openly and honestly with his or her disability and find ways to transcend its inherent limitations. One must master the emotional and attitudinal barriers that accompany the stereotypes constructed over time immemorial, and one must learn the knowledge and skills that every person needs to claim a spot in the game of life. The stories that I tell trace the overcoming of these challenges in everyday life. My goal is to inform, but if the reader gathers a deeper appreciation for the value of life from my affirmations, I will be pleased, for I ground my life and struggles in the strongly held belief that life is valuable and fully participating in it is the best way to experience the joy of living.

These stories are not tales of easy triumph or fantasies of shallow, happy success. They are narratives of hard work and disappointment, accomplishment and failure, happiness and despair. They are the stories of real people who live in the real world, who claim their places in the face of real challenges, and who affirm life in full awareness of its capacity to have a dark side.

This project has taken many years to come to fruition. It began fifteen years ago, when my wife and I initiated the publication of a magazine that we called *Disability Life*. We wanted to share the lives of persons with disabilities with a larger reading public. We published *DL* for over a year, until we ran out of funds, but rearmed with enthusiasm, advanced technology, and some innovations in the publishing business, we are ready to try again.

On January 11, 1989, I took the oath of office and became a Boulder County Commissioner. During the previous fifteen years, I had lived and worked in Boulder County, Colorado. I had involved myself in the life of the community and won enough trust and respect from the voting public to win election in a countywide race with an incumbent commissioner. Among the issues that I discussed with the public was that of my blindness. The question was, of course, could a blind person perform all the tasks demanded by the office? Could a blind person review maps, development plans, and complex financial reports? My opponent did not think so and tried to make it an issue, but I won. The voters had given me an opportunity to prove that a blind person could serve effectively in the office, and I welcomed the challenge.

Blindness is thought by many to be a severely disabling condition. Once, while I rode a city bus, a man told me that he would rather be dead than to be blind. Scholars have asserted blindness is a tragedy, a spoiled identity, or even a justifiable cause for taking one's own life. Our language uses *blind* as a synonym for unthinking, a stubborn refusal for seeing the truth, a lack of clarity, or complete irrationality. People with limited vision are encouraged to hide their impairment, lest they be viewed as blind. All too often professional educators and rehabilitation workers accept the negative definition of blindness that our culture maintains. Yet blind men and women make good lives for themselves, find ways to be productive, and make significant contributions to their families and communities. My story traces my path as I worked to establish a healthy, positive sense of self-worth and to redefine the meaning of blindness for myself and for my community.

For at least five generations, blindness has been a characteristic of many of my family members. During the last century and a half, we have been farmers, housewives, construction workers, teachers, landladies, Sunday schoolteachers, and college professors. My mother sewed in a garment factory, my cousin moved houses, and I served as an elected member of the Boulder County Board of Commissioners. Each of the blind members of my family worked and contributed to his or her home and family. While many went through hard times, each one found ways to survive and be productive. For the most part, we lacked education and specialized skills. We lived through war and depression. We had little backing or family wealth. What we had was pride, determination, and a willingness to work, and most importantly, we refused to believe that we were marginal people who needed others to care for us.

The particular form of blindness that occurs in our family is retinitis pigmentosa (RP). This condition affects the retina of the eye. Usually a child will have enough vision to function relatively normally during the early years, but by adolescence or early adulthood, one's vision begins to fail. The condition progresses until by midlife, the individual experiences legal or even total blindness. Early symptoms include night blindness, a blurring of sight, and a loss of central vision. Many who have RP start life as if they had normal vision. They learn to read print, play games, and even drive a car, but as the disease progresses, they must give up these activities. It is often hard for them to accept the loss of vision that they are experiencing. It can be especially difficult for them to employ alternative techniques, such as using a white cane, learning Braille, or giving up driving a car. Members of my family have struggled with the progressive nature of RP with differing results and adaptations. To my knowledge, I have been the family member with the least vision from early childhood. I have often thought of this as a blessing, because I never pretended that I could see more than I really could. I always functioned as a blind person and developed my adaptations from early childhood.

I am a part of a family with important stories to tell. They are stories of persons who took whatever they had to work with and made a life. We are not famous or significant in any larger sense, but we have refused to take a backseat in life. We insist that we are players who control our own destinies, at least as much as anyone else does. While others may have told us that we could, often even should, get out of the way and let others care for us and direct our lives, we rejected the offer, quietly but decisively in the only way that counts. We did things, we acted, and we performed. We did not ask permission or wait for approval. We just married, farmed, went to school, and made ourselves valuable to whatever enterprise we were committed to. We are people of humble means, but we are tough and we have a great deal of determination. Perhaps my story can help others to understand what it means to be blind or to have a disability; I hope that it will shine some light on the basic human need to be useful and productive. I do not think that human beings can be happy if they do not believe that they are of value to others. We insist that the world is ours as much as anyone's to enjoy, to direct, or to have it break our hearts.

When I was a child, we lived near a limestone rock quarry. The quarry produced lime to fertilize the fields in the community and to make the cement that built the roads and buildings throughout the county. It was dangerous work, and over the years, a number of men lost their lives in the explosions that broke up the rock. The death of one such unfortunate man made a lasting impression on me and remains a permanent metaphor in my mental furnishings. I am not sure if my understanding of what happened is true or if I constructed the story to fit my need for a narrative that would support what I already believed to be true. As the years have passed, I have come to believe that my needs shaped the interpretation of the facts. No matter, the story as I understand it states well the meaning of life as we lived it.

One morning the men were blasting in the quarry. Too late one of the workers recognized that he was too close to a blast site. A rope strung across a chasm offered a possible escape. He tried to swing himself over the hole, but the exploding rock hit one of his arms, breaking it. He held on until a second rock broke his other arm. He fell and was killed. I never saw this horrible accident as a tragedy. As a child, I saw it as an act of courage. The man never gave up. He kept fighting for his life, even though the odds were stacked against him. He tried to escape, and when he was injured, he still kept fighting. The incident became a metaphor for determination. I never thought about his losing the struggle; I only thought about his ferocious will to live. In later years, I have recognized the certainty of losing the battle, but I still applaud the struggle. It is the only way to live.

My grandmother's full name was Annie Mary Krumes Creech. She was born in 1883 and died in 1955. My memory of her dates from a time when she was in her sixties. My best memories came after she had her first stroke and was only a greatly reduced version of the attractive, forceful woman that she had been throughout her life. Still, her stories and her determination, even in illness, to be productive made a lasting impression on the child that I was at the time.

She was an old lady, my grandmother, but she had not always been that person. Her wedding picture shows an attractive, dark-haired woman, youthful and happy. She grew up in the little village of Old Alexandria, near Troy, Missouri, in Lincoln County. Her home set across a gravel road from the Methodist Church, where she met Vada Creech, a neighbor boy, who became her husband. She lived with her widowed mother, Elizabeth Krumes, a blind woman, and her three sisters—one of whom, Emmy, was also blind. Annie attended a one-room school in her neighborhood, where she learned the basics and developed a lifelong belief that she was an excellent student. The world that she grew up in demanded less of vision than does today's world. She had little need to read much printed material, nor did she need to drive a car. Her work involved caring for children, doing housework, working in her yard and garden, and participating in the life of her church. She had enough functional vision to carry out her tasks without many accommodations until her stroke caused a significant loss of sight. Only then did she find her blindness to limit her life activities, although her vision had been substantially impaired decades before.

It is difficult for a contemporary person to understand what life was like in rural America before electricity reached the houses and the gasoline engine powered the farm equipment. The power to do the work came from horses and the men and women who wrestled a living from the land. An entire life could be spent within a few miles of the homestead. One might take only a few trips of fifty miles or more during his or her whole life. One lived surrounded by relatives. Parents divided land among their children, and generations of kin lived within a short walk from one another. One found respect by what one did. A man kept his buildings, equipment, and animals in good shape. He planted, weeded, and harvested his crops on time, his fences were in repair, and his family was well-fed, clothed, and behaved. A woman's house was clean, and her husband and children wore clean clothing, which was in good repair. Her food was well prepared, and the pies and cakes that she took to church affairs were tasty. A blind woman carved out her place in her family and community as did every other woman, by performing successfully in the role that she inherited. Annie did what was expected of her and more.

Annie had little trouble seeing in her early life. She worked intermittently as a maid before her marriage and moved into the adult role of wife with ease. Her vision began to present problems when she was in her thirties. She needed to use a magnifying glass to read the Sunday schoolbook that she used to teach her class. Still, she had little trouble with cooking and cleaning, washing and gardening, canning and sewing. She was a leader at her church, an appreciated cook; she kept a good house and managed her family well. Her vision did not cause real problems until her fifties.

Vada died in 1937. It was the depression, and Annie and her daughter were in danger of losing their home because they could not pay the taxes. They needed income. They connected with the St. Louis Department of Family Services. Annie in her 50's and her daughter, D'arline, in her 20's, became foster parents for several foster children. Annie could not see to do the paperwork for the department, so her daughter handled this part of the job. Together they provided a home for a number of children for several years.

When D'arline married and her husband joined the army, Annie did the farmwork, while D'arline cared for her two small sons. Annie was in her sixties and her vision was failing, but she did the work. She fed the horses and cows, milked and fed the chickens, and carried water. They put in a garden and did the housework. By this time, Annie could not see to read, but she could still thread a needle and she mended the children's clothing.

A few years later, Annie had a stroke, which caused her to lose her remaining sight and to experience physically disabling symptoms. Nevertheless, she continued to help as she could. She helped to care for D'arline's new baby, prepared fruit and vegetables for cooking and canning, and helped with the dishes. She looked for chances to help and did what she could.

As Annie aged, she lost sight. Her world was not very dependent on vision, however, and she made few accommodations. She continued to do what life demanded of her and had no thought of giving up her role as wife, mother, and family and community leader. Even in old age, she looked for ways to be useful. She never gave up believing that she could be a useful person. She worked hard throughout her life. She took responsibility and demanded that others pay attention to her directions. She was a smart, wise, and tough woman who was proud and determined. In the time and place in which she lived, she could accommodate to the loss of sight with minimal adjustments. She never accepted blindness as a cause for retiring from the struggle to be a responsible, productive member of her world.

My mother, D'arline Creech Page, was Annie's second child. Born in 1915, she lived until 1998. D'arline was a timid woman. Her mother was controlling, and D'arline always resented her domination. She was fearful and dependent. She never took a leadership role in her community as did her mother. She was in poor health for most of her life; yet she anchored her family.

D'arline was the first member of her family to attend high school. However, she dropped out after the tenth grade. Perhaps she was too shy to make friends in the larger consolidated high school—she had attended a one-room school through the first eight grades—or perhaps her limited vision held her back. She could not see the blackboard or keep up with the reading. She developed headaches from eyestrain. In the end, she chose the safer and more comfortable path of dropping out and waiting at home for life to find her. Her father died, and she and her mother scrambled to survive in the hard times of the Great Depression. She learned to drive a car and provided transportation for herself and her mother, at least during the day. She could not drive at night. She and her mother continued to care for foster children until the birth of her first child.

In 1940, she married Homer Page. Homer grew up on a neighboring farm, but his parents died when he was a child, and he bounced around among relatives and friends of the family. He joined the New Deal Civilian Conservation Corps, worked as a farmhand, traveled the rodeo circuit as a rodeo cowboy, and played his guitar in the streets and bars of St. Louis. He needed to settle down, find a home, and marry a woman who was not threatening, someone who would depend on him and be devoted to him. D'arline needed a husband who could bring meaning and excitement into her life. She gave him stability. He gave her a normal life, in which she could be a normal woman. Her family became her vocation.

D'arline gave birth to two sons, and then nine years later, she had a daughter. Annie lived with the family, and the two women worked together to do the work of the household. They cleaned and cooked, washed clothes by hand in a washtub, carried water, planted and cared for a large garden, canned the fruit and vegetables, and cared for the children. D'arline worked for a short time in a garment factory in town and made most of the clothing for the children until they were old enough to go to school. She took the cloth from feed sacks, dyed the material, and sewed shirts for her sons and dresses for herself and her mother. The family lived on the same farm where she was born, and her sons were born there as well. In this familiar environment, her impaired sight made little difference. She knew how to do her work. She knew where everything was located, and her sight was adequate to read what little print she needed to process. It was a safe, comfortable, although limited life, and she did her share and more.

John Delmar Creech, Uncle Delmar, was Annie's oldest child. Born in 1912, he grew up on the family farm. He learned to handle a team of horses, raise hogs and cattle, grow a crop, and manage a farm. He worked with his father and won the reputation of being an excellent field hand. Even in his nineties, he proudly told stories of picking corn as an adolescent and keeping up with the fastest men. He married, and he and his wife raised two sons. He farmed his entire life, keeping hogs into his eighties.

Uncle Delmar played an important role in my life. He was my closest male relative who was blind. He had some usable sight into his midlife, but by his forties, he had very little vision. I watched his progress

11

through life. Although I never had as much vision as he had in his younger years, I knew that I would, as did Uncle Delmar, lose what vision I did have. He was interesting to me because he demonstrated that I could continue to function well after my sight was completely gone. He continued to farm and manage his life. He remained happy and optimistic, and while I was not going to be a farmer, I recognized that life would go on after I was totally blind. I observed Uncle Delmar and realized that I need not fear total blindness.

Blindness was a characteristic of many of the people with whom I grew up. It was a topic about which little was said. Everyone defined himself or herself by what he or she did, and what they did was work and play, raise children and pay their taxes, love and argue, and do the normal, everyday things that men and women who were their peers did. Each person contributed. No one was pitied; no one was let off easy. Blind or sighted, everyone did his or her job.

The world into which I was born was a simple one. No one had high expectations. No one attended college, had a professional occupation, or achieved even a middle-class lifestyle. There were few heart-wrenching doubts about the future of a blind child. Other family members were blind, and they were all right, so why not the newest one? The ambiguities of the blindness role confronted me only later in life. I faced the negativity of the larger society when I went to school, but my family was not torn by the dark doubts of a more sophisticated social order. Our values were straightforward. Each person is to be a contributing, productive person, and it is up to the family to see that a blind child learns to play his or her part in the well-being of the family. Although I did not learn an appreciation for fine literature or music, inherit material goods, or learn how to survive in a postindustrial society, I did learn that I was a valuable member of our family. I learned my blindness was no reason to sit on the sidelines of life and that a blind person could and should take responsibility for himself or herself and for those with whom he or she lived. In the totality of things, I believe that I was very fortunate, indeed, to have the family that I did and to internalize the values that my family gave to me.

CHAPTER 2

The Hill: The Making of a Blind Child

T HE HILL COUNTRY AROUND TROY, Missouri, is poor farming land, and the Great Depression of the 1930s did not end there until the 1950s. It was an inauspicious place to grow up, but it was where I was born and lived during the 1940s and '50s, until I went to college in 1959. Fortunately for me, the very land and the people who lived on it provided me with the education in life that I needed to make my way in a much more complicated world.

During the years of my childhood, my family lived in a condition of respectable poverty. We had neither electricity nor running water in our home. The crops failed regularly. Cattle prices were too low to make a profit on the animals that we sent to market. We lived on the food we grew in our garden, the animals that we butchered, the chickens that we kept, and the seasonal employment that my father found after he returned from the army in 1946. Everyone in the family worked to squeeze our livelihood from the soil, but so did the families living on neighboring farms, so no one felt especially disadvantaged. Hard work and character, not material goods, marked a successful family, and by that measure, our family was as successful as any.

My family was unique in some ways, however. A number of us were blind. Retinitis pigmentosa is a hereditary condition that causes blindness, and it affected members of my family for at least five generations. I inherited this condition, and it has, of course, played a major role in shaping my

13

life. Growing up with others who were blind and observing them make successful lives gave me adult models from which to learn. Engaging the challenges and adventures of the land where I grew up allowed me to develop the confidence, personal strength, endurance, and optimism that I have needed to create a far different life than the one into which I was born.

One learns that when the crops fail, the only option is to plant again in the spring; and when the cattle prices break the hearts of the family, the only alternative is to buy more calves to feed for next year. The garden must be planted, the potatoes dug, the chickens fed, and the cow milked, and the only ones to do it are the members of the family. It does not matter if some of them are blind; the work needs to be done, so, blind or not, they do it. For a blind child, doing the work is an exercise in self-affirmation. It was always a source of joy for me to make a genuine contribution to the work of the family. I knew that I was valuable, and that did more to help me grow than could all the luxury in the world.

The story that I have to tell is one of ambition and disappointment, failure and growth, self-acceptance and frustration. It is the story of a blind boy and man who was eager to embrace the opportunities and challenges of life, confront and accept the limitations that are grounded in his blindness and also those that simply exist because he is a human being, and keep playing when the game of life gets hard. My story is one of affirmation in the face of challenge and defeat; no defeat is permanent and no challenge is destructive if they are used as tools for growth, learning, and adaptation. I have made a valuable life, not in spite of being blind, but rather with blindness as one of the conditions of my life. I have not overcome my blindness. I have allowed it to be a part of who I am. It is a characteristic of me, just as are all the others that make me the person that I am.

Lincoln County, where I grew up, is north of St. Louis. Its eastern border is the Mississippi River. The Quiver River cuts diagonally across the county from northwest to southeast, emptying into the Mississippi near

Old Monroe. Many small branches and creeks drain the hill country along the Quiver and flow into it. The farm where I lived for the first fifteen years of my life was bisected by one of these tiny branches. It ran intermittently at the bottom of a deep ravine, which was formed by two steep sides. Much of my early years were spent along the branch and on the hills of this modest geological feature. The branch came on to our property along its northern fence line and flowed south. The eastern slope was somewhat longer and less steep than was the western side. The west slope was very steep, rising to a flat plain, where the fields lay. The county road ran at the top of the eastern slope, and a gravel road ran from the county's road to our house. Our road cut perpendicularly across the ravine. Coming onto our property, one would pass down the eastern slope, and then face a steep incline that was a challenge to an automobile, bicycle, person, or horse wishing to climb to the top. At the top of the hill set our house, barn, and other outbuildings. Three generations of blind people created their lives on the eighty acres that formed the poor dirt farm at the top of the hill.

The autumn of 1941 was one of the wettest in history. The Cuivre River went over its banks, flooding the rich bottomland along its course through Lincoln County. The small branch at the bottom of the hill became a raging torrent, washing out the culvert in the road, making it impassable. My father was a horse trainer, and that fall he had taken a horse to break that was especially wild. A week before the big flood, he had ridden the horse to town, and on the way home, it slipped on the highway and fell. His leg was pinned beneath the animal and broken. My father's accident, coupled with the flood, presented my family with a serious problem. My mother was nine months pregnant. She planned to deliver at home, but if the bridge were not repaired, the doctor could not get to the house. Together, my father and mother managed to get down the hill with enough materials and tools to repair the washed-out culvert, allowing the doctor to reach our house and assist as I made my appearance into the world.

D'Arline Creech Page was born on September 12, 1915, on the same farm. The house in which she was born burned in 1933. She and her mother were washing clothes when the fire that heated the water in the big iron kettle got out of control and caught the house on fire. They had neither water nor help to fight the fire, and the house burned to the ground. The new house was roughly a thirty- by thirty-foot-square building, with a porch across the front and a utility room and screened-in porch attached to the rear. My grandfather died soon after the fire, and my mother and grandmother lived together in the new house until my mother and father were married.

Both my mother and my grandmother were blind. They maintained the farm, had a few cows and chickens, and cared for foster children to make ends meet. The home did not have running water, indoor plumbing, or electricity; yet these two blind women cared for several orphan children and managed a farm. This was the Great Depression, and they lived in what we would consider today to be rural poverty, but it was normal to them. Nursing an injured husband, repairing a washed-out road, and bearing a child were just the demands of the day, and they were perfectly competent to satisfy those demands. The courage, endurance, and creativity of those simple country folk set the social context in which I was to come of age. Blindness was not a reason for sitting on the sideline of life. Everyone needed to contribute and too much needed to be done, so even a small boy was not excused. The flood was just a reminder that when things need to be done, there is just one way to meet the challenge: one must scramble down the hill with a shovel and put the gravel back on the road.

My brother, Harold, was two years younger than I. For many years, we played on the hill and up and down the branch as it flowed through our farm. Sometimes we played together, and at other times, we played by ourselves. We played army and cowboys, using sticks for rifles and broomsticks for horses. We sledded in the winter snow, and my brother dug a hideout in the side of the hill. I ran up the hill in training for an imaginary Olympic gold medal. We rode our horses and herded calves up and down the slopes. We had few toys or tools, but our imaginations were unlimited.

One of the things that my brother and I enjoyed was playing in the water in the branch. There were two holes where the water was perhaps eighteen inches deep. These were our swimming holes, until we got old enough to go to a pond that was a mile from our farm. We caught frogs and pretended to swim. Since we did not have running water in our house, these playful outings were also what passed for baths during the summer months. On occasion, we even took soap along with us, although my memory is hazy about whether or not it was ever used.

Play was not without its risk. Old Dan was a big white horse who was mine to ride. One Sunday morning after church, friends of our family stopped for Sunday dinner. Their son, Hurley, a boy five years younger than I, and I were riding Old Dan. We were riding bareback. We had ridden to the county road on the eastern side of the ravine, and when we started up the hill going to the house, I kicked Dan into a gallop. Neither of us could remember what happened then, but we slid off and were knocked unconscious. Each of us got up and walked to the house, but we were completely unaware of doing it. We never received medical treatment, but undoubtedly we had concussions. We spent several days recovering.

On another occasion, I left the house to ride my bicycle to the mailbox at the county road. As I went down the hill, I tried to pick up speed to be able to ride up the other side, but the bicycle wheel hit loose gravel and I was thrown off. I broke my arm, and for the first time in my life, I went to the hospital, to have the bone set. This was a particularly bitter accident, because we were planning to go the next day to an amusement park in St. Louis, where the major attraction was a roller coaster.

Although I was blind, my parents gave me the freedom and encouragement to do the normal things the other boys my age did. I learned to manage a horse, ride a bicycle, and run, wrestle, and play boys' games. Occasionally I got banged up, but so did other kids my age. Had my parents been more protective, I may have escaped a broken bone and some bumps and bruises, but the price that I would have paid would have been very high. In addition to the life-long benefits to my health from a childhood of exercise, I learned that I could play with others as a normal person. I did not sit on the sidelines while others played. I learned what my limits were, but no one artificially set those limits. The lessons that I learned on my playground taught me to engage my world, not retire from it. It was not the dependent blindness role, but one of adaptation and involvement that I learned on the hill.

When a farmhouse lacks a constant supply of water, the entire family is enlisted in a daily effort to provide this essential element of human and animal life. My earliest memories of work revolve around the daily carrying of water to our house and to the chickens and hogs that we kept. A cistern well was located at the corner of the house that was filled by runoff from the roof, but the well leaked and would go dry during the summer. My mother sent me to the well with a three-gallon bucket to bring water. The well had a pump, which in the beginning, I had to use both hands to turn. I could only carry a half-full bucket, so this meant that I had to make several trips to get enough water for household use. While runoff from one side of the house filled the well, the runoff from the other side filled tubs and large jars with the water needed to wash the clothes and mop the floors. Water was also carried from these receptacles to the chicken house. I helped my mother and grandmother in caring for the chickens.

Capturing rainwater worked much of the time, but during dry periods, it was inadequate to meet our family needs. During those times, we turned to the springs that fed the branch at the bottom of the hill. We used two of these springs. One flowed directly under the hill below the house, and the other lay a few hundred yards downstream. The first was closer, but the second lasted longer. My brother, Harold, and I were often sent to the spring to get water. We would have to team up to carry a single bucket, but since I was taller, the bucket tilted toward my brother and the water would splash out on him. We tried to fill the bucket as full as we could to minimize our trips, but this added to the splashing and to the arguing between the two of us. Still, we carried water for the house and to Irl and Maggie, two pigs that we raised for meat. We carried water until 1952, when electricity reached our farm and a deep well could be drilled to a permanent water supply; an electric pump made running water possible in our house and barnyard. I was eleven years old at the time, and my brother was nine.

The slopes on either side of the ravine were too steep to mow with the horse-drawn mower that my father used to keep the weeds down on our farm. Each evening when my father returned from his maintenance job at a nearby summer camp, he would assign the location on the hill where Harold and I were to cut the weeds on the next day. He would assess our work, and if we had left any standing, he would point them out and we would have to cut them the next morning.

We used a small scythe called a reaphook. It was hard, hot work cutting weeds in the summer sun, but cutting weeds was not as hard for me as finding them. I would take a stick and swing it around me, looking for standing weeds. This proved rather effective, although not quite perfect, and I would often be forced to go over again my assigned areas to complete the job. While this was frustrating and I often felt sorry for myself, I learned that excuses did little good. It is important to be thorough and take the time to do a complete job the first time. My father's demanding standards were high, and he saw that I fulfilled his expectations.

Harold and I often worked with our father on Saturday mornings during the school year. He would cut sprouts with an ax, and we would pile them in brush piles for later burning. At other times, we would help him build and repair fences or haul gravel from a creek two miles away. He would talk with us and give us our basic education in sexuality, farm management, and the ways of being men. He also taught us to dream. On one of these outings, he asked us if we would like to sponsor a rodeo on our farm. He said that we needed to build a rodeo arena and explained to us what to do. We were excited about the prospect and readily assented to the proposition. We knew that we could do it, because he had been a rodeo cowboy in his youth, and when he and our mother were first married, he had given two rodeos on our farm to make enough money to pay the back taxes. It was, after all, the time of the Great Depression in rural America.

The first task was to cut the trees to split into posts to make the arena. The woods from which we cut the trees covered the slopes along the branch. At first, our father worked with us. He taught us to use a tape measure to determine if a tree were large enough to make posts. Then, we learned to notch a tree with an ax to make it fall in the right direction, and then to use a hand-drawn saw to cut the tree. The saw required a person on either end to saw back and forth across the timber. The two needed to work in harmony to keep the teeth sliding through the wood without binding. The saw had to be kept level and straight. He worked with each of us, in turn, while we learned the basic skills. Later we worked alone on days that he was at work.

At times, the saw would bind. In most cases, it was my fault, because I could not see the blade and I had to keep my end level by the feel as the blade cut through the wood. Still, we enjoyed working for a common goal and improved our technique with practice. Harold was unusually tolerant of my shortcomings for a child of perhaps eleven, and because I was older and larger, I took on most of the heavy lifting. When a fallen tree needed to be moved, we would trim the limbs, measure the length of the posts along the tree trunk, and saw through it, leaving a post length to be hauled to the arena location, where our father would split it into posts. Later, we learned to dig postholes and set the posts in line for boards to be nailed to them to make the rodeo arena.

The work on the corral was fun and exciting. It gave us a chance to test our growing strength and win our father's approval. However, one day our work came to a quick and painful end. We cut down a tree, but it did not fall in the direction that we planned; instead, it fell and caught on another tree. We climbed the standing tree to saw off a limb and let the cut tree fall to the ground, but unbeknownst to us, a hornets' nest hid in the tree. When we began to saw the limb, the hornets flew out of their nest and attacked us with fury. We exited the tree with dispatch and ran as fast as we could, but the hornets chased us and we each received over seventy stings. Each sting swelled and created intense pain. The venom from the insects made us very sick, putting an end to our cutting for several days while our bodies processed the poison. I have had a life-long reaction to insect stings since this incident. When we went back to the woods, we checked very carefully to determine if there were hornets, wasps, or yellow jackets nearby.

I learned to work and play, make accommodations for my blindness, accept my limits, and find ways to make essential contributions to shared undertakings on the hill in front of our house. The ravine and the slopes that made it challenged and disciplined me as I grew into adolescence. I measured my strength and skill against the hill as I rode a bicycle, carried a larger and larger bucket of water, or cut and hauled a tree. I learned to find weeds, using a technique that would help me in adulthood to use a long white cane to travel independently throughout the world. I accepted the need to let my brother do the things that required sight, such as measuring the size of a tree with a tape measure or sighting the placement of a posthole to create a straight line of posts, but I also found ways to use my strength and determination to push forward a job to its conclusion. I learned that pain, frustration, and even injury should not prevent me from carrying through on my plans. On that hill, I learned to imagine, to dream and to plan, to trust my associates and to work together for a common goal. I learned to be tough, optimistic, and resilient. These are lessons that have enriched my life and allowed me to challenge the blindness role that often ruins the identity of a blind person.

During the first fifteen years of my life, while my family lived on the hill, four persons dominated my attention. There were others—cousins, neighborhood children, adult relatives, and visitors—but my mother, father, grandmother, and brother filled my social world, and they formed my basic values and approach to life. They cared for me, directed my actions, disciplined me, challenged me to live up to a set of high expectations, and gave me the space to explore my capacities, imagination, and independence. While the location and circumstances of my childhood were extremely limited, the social environment was affirmative, challenging, and expansive. The people on the hill encouraged me to be physically and emotionally strong, to enjoy taking risks, and to be self-directed and independent. I shall be grateful to

21

them as long as I live for the acceptance and ease with which they allowed me to be a normal child.

While I was growing up, my family attended the Old Alexandria Methodist Church, a small rural church in a nearby village. The army drafted my father when I was three years old. One Sunday while he was gone, I went to church with my mother and grandmother. During the sermon, I got up and ran outside. My grandmother went after me, and when she caught me, she took me behind the woodshed and gave me a spanking. We went back inside, and I sat quietly through the rest of the service. The next Sunday I sat attentively until the minister began to preach about a man who stood up on his housetop to see Jesus. I stood up in disbelief and shouted, "He stood up on top of the house?" This time I was hushed but not spanked. They preferred to have me listen and comment, rather than to run out of the church. They told the story over and over, but in a way that let me know that they appreciated my attentive, yet critical, question. It is a lesson that I have taken with me throughout my life.

During the year that I was four, I broke my arm twice. The first time my mother was sewing on a foot-driven treadle machine. When she finished, she folded the machine back into its storage position and started to roll it back into the utility room. My brother and I asked to ride on the top of the machine. She set us on it, but I chose to try to ride while standing up. I fell and broke my arm. Several months later, my mother and grandmother were washing clothes on a washboard. The floor on the back porch was wet, and I slipped and fell out the porch door, breaking my arm again.

I was young and the bones healed quickly, but while my arm was in a cast, I hounded my mother and grandmother to teach me the Twenty-Third Psalm and the Pledge of Allegiance. An older cousin was learning these pieces in school, and I wanted to know them as well as he did. They drilled me until I learned to say them, and then, when my aunts and uncles came to visit from St. Louis, I would recite them, often being rewarded with compliments and nickels and dimes, and even once with a quarter. The family told me that I was a stubborn and smart little boy, and I liked both contributions to my growing sense of self.

When my father returned from the army in 1946, when I was almost five years old, our family life picked up where it left off when the military drafted him. I recall nights sitting on his lap, listening to the Lone Ranger on the radio, and during commercial breaks getting down on the floor to do push-ups. I did sixty pushups each night. I loved being with my dad, and these evenings were wonderful. When young adult relatives would come to visit, Dad would challenge them to have a push-up contest with me. Since I was six or seven years old, they readily assented, but much to their surprise, I always won. My father got a big laugh out of the contest, and I was elated, both from the pleasure of winning and from the approval it gained for me from my father.

Throughout my childhood, a favorite activity of my father's was horseback riding with his children. When I was six, we had a horse whose name was Old Queen. She was over twenty, but still with some spirit and an aggressive nature. Old Queen was mine to ride. I listened with my father to the running of the Kentucky Derby and begged to take my horse to the derby. My father asked me if I would like to race him on his horse. This seemed to me like a wonderful sporting event. There was a level space at the top of the hill lying just south of the barn lot. Years later, we built the rodeo corral in this area. We rode our horses to the edge of the woods at the top of the hill and turned them toward the barn. My father said, "Go!" and I kicked Old Queen into a gallop, but she did not want to race. She began to buck in an effort to throw me. I held on tight and finished the ride to the barn. While we never took Old Queen to the Kentucky Derby, I received many compliments for my ride, and I felt like a hero for weeks to come.

During the summer that I was eight, my ego received a powerful affirmation. I was helping my father put a new roof on the chicken house. I held down the roll of tar paper, and he nailed it to the building. The roof was slanted at a rather steep angle, but I felt comfortable and enjoyed working with my dad. As we were working, I heard a car climb the hill, and I could smell the dust. Two persons, a man and a woman, stepped out of the car and introduced themselves. They were from the Missouri School for the Blind.

We stayed on the roof. My mother came out and offered our visitors a glass of tea. They told us that they would like me to attend their school. They said that I could learn things that would help me adjust to my blindness. My father was polite, but he let them know that he and my mother were not interested in my going away to school. He gave them three very good reasons. "First," he said, "a boy's place is at home with his family; and second, he is doing fine in school; and third [and this was the one that meant the most to me], who will help me with all this work if he is off somewhere in school?" They got back in their car and left. We never heard from the school again.

This was the most affirming event of my childhood. My parents said that they loved me and wanted me at home, that I was successful in school, and that they needed me to help with the work. I felt completely secure in my place with my family. I have often thought about that affirmation. It was powerful because a great deal was at risk for me. I did not want to leave my home. I also believed that it was true. My family did love me. I was doing well in school, and I did do a lot of work. While I was blind, so were my mother and grandmother, and we each contributed to the family well-being and livelihood. No one had to convince anyone of the productivity of blind persons. One need only observe who did the work.

I did well in school, but doing homework was a struggle. I could not see to read, so I needed help from my parents. My mother could read, with difficulty, the larger print in the books they used in the lower grades, but soon she had to stop helping me. My father enjoyed reading some of the books, but not all. I particularly remember the winter of my sixth grade. We were required to read and pass a quiz on twenty library books. During the evenings, he would read from these books to the entire family. We sat around the stove in the living room; sometimes my mother would make popcorn, and he would read. I was always prepared for the quiz on the book. That year I read more books than anyone in my class did. My father's help with homework ended two years later, when he took a job working at night and was no longer at home in the evenings.

My parents were not educated people. My father dropped out of school in the eighth grade and my mother after the tenth. Yet they wanted me to succeed in school and helped as best they could. I learned that if I had access to print materials, I could do very well, indeed, and if I did not, I could do as well as my classmates. I was in graduate school before I got consistent access to print, and it changed the opportunities for my life and career. The new technology made recorded materials available, and the outstanding work of organizations such as Recordings for the Blind and Dyslexic produced a library of books that have aided countless numbers of blind students over the last half century. Contemporary computer-based technology has expanded enormously the availability of print material for blind persons. I have benefited immensely from the technological advances of the last fifty years, but the idea that education and learning could be a way of life that I could pursue began with my parents reading to me in the evenings on the hill.

My grandmother lived with us for most of the time, but she would visit her son's family for several weeks each year. I spent a great deal of time with her as a small child, and she was a second mother to me. She had been a strong woman throughout her life, managing her home, raising her children, teaching Sunday school, and scraping together a living after her husband's death. When my parents married, my father moved into her house. When he went to the army, she did the farmwork, while my mother, who was in poor health, took care of two small children. She disciplined and cared for me, and I was much attached to her. When I was nine years old, she had a stroke, which largely ended her active life. For the next five years, until her death, she was an invalid. She sat in an old wooden rocking chair and did what she could to help. When my sister was born, she would hold her; and she would help with the peeling and slicing of fruit and vegetables for canning, but she needed help walking.

I spent many hours sitting on the floor at my grandmother's feet. We talked, and she told me the family stories. She told me of her feelings of uselessness and of what she took to be neglect by her children. We did not have an indoor bathroom, so I would walk with her to the outhouse. This required getting down, and then back up, three large steps off the back porch. I was nervous about these trips, but we never had an accident on the steps. I learned to be patient with my grandmother and to never betray her feelings to others. My parents complimented me for my care for her, and I felt affirmed by their remarks. I learned to care for and about another person from these years with my grandmother. I took on responsibilities that were demanding for a child my age, but they were not beyond my capacities and I grew from the trust placed in me.

When I was fifteen, our family moved to another farm, which was larger and more productive. It represented another dream of my father's: to become a bigger and better farmer, and to engage his sons in a larger challenge. It turned out to be a short-term success, for in two years I would leave for college, never to return to the family enterprise, and in another two years, my brother would leave to pursue his own goals. The two years spent on the new farm were years of growth and challenge, but they were, for the most part, years of transition between my life on the hill and a life in the larger world. It was the first fifteen years that defined me and helped to set my course as an adult.

The person who I was becoming instinctively rejected the negativity associated with the limitations of the blindness role. My parents instilled a sense of personal worth and security into my deepest being. They had taught me to be productive and expected me to perform at a high level. They encouraged me to be physically and emotionally strong, to be willing to take risks, and to follow my dreams. They demanded that I assume responsibility for others and for myself, and they allowed me the freedom to define myself as a person and, especially, as a blind man. The hill may not have been the best playground and workshop for a boy to have, but it was good for me. The people on the hill may not have been the most sophisticated or educated, but they knew what it meant to be proud, self-reliant men and women, and they passed their knowledge on to their children.

By the time I left the hill, I was prepared to take my place in a changing world. I could reject the blindness role and make it stick. I was ready to take advantage of the changes that were going to give people who are blind and disabled opportunities that never existed before. After World War II, a new generation of persons with disabilities emerged, who combined the resilience of traditional values with the opportunities provided by new technologies, new rehabilitation and educational opportunities, and new advocacy and civil rights. The making of this new generation has transformed the thinking about blindness and has made older stereotypes profoundly obsolete.

A widely read book written by Princeton sociologist Robert Scott, entitled *The Making of Blind Men*, did much to shape the thinking of professionals working in the field of blindness. Scott thought that most blind persons conformed to a social role that their blindness defined. One of the more disparaging passages in Scott's text describes the imagined interview that a blind man has with a potential employer. Scott focused on the uncertainty and discomfort of the employer and the incompetence of the blind applicant. It is no wonder that Scott's blind man failed to get the job. In this scenario, the blind man cannot find an ashtray, drops ashes on his suit, and lacks the ability to put his interviewer at ease. He is not a confident, highly skilled person who would be an asset to the employer's organization. To Scott's way of thinking, such a blind man simply did not exist. His imagined scenario sets the tone for his analysis. Perhaps the most frustrating aspect of a blind person's life is the imagined incompetence that he or she faces from others. Yet this prejudgment does not define who we are.

In high school, I wanted to take a typing class. The teacher expressed her concern about how I would know what to type. "The students type from a copybook," she said. "How will you know what to type?"

I told her that I would just make up things. I told her, "People always tell me no. They say that I can't do things, but I do them anyhow." One can define oneself by rejecting roles imposed by society. However, one does not create an identity in a vacuum. It is necessary to have love and support and authentic experience, which can provide the foundation for an alternative identity. For many, if not most, blind and disabled persons, those resources are available to them. I had them in abundance. Unfortunately, too much of the research and writing on blindness and disability focuses on the deficits associated with the disability, not on the resources and accommodations that one can draw upon to forge a healthy identity. Our research and writing needs to focus on what makes blind people successful. In my case, the hill and the people on it gave me the personal resources that I needed to reject Scott's blindness role and create a satisfying and productive life. Large numbers of similar narratives are waiting to be told. May disabled people tell their stories with pride and insight, and may their stories be told in abundance!

CHAPTER 3

School Days

I BEGAN SCHOOL IN THE fall of 1947. Troy Elementary School was an old brick building, built in 1896. I spent the next six years in its classrooms and on its playground, learning to get along with the other children, to adjust to my blindness, and to assert myself on occasion. The students and teachers accepted me into the life of the school. In some cases, they changed the rules to let me play. Often other children, or even the teachers, would read materials to me, and at times, I dealt with heartbreaking disappointment. I learned that no one can do everything, so each person, including me, must find those affirming things that he or she can do, and then learn to love and market them. I look back on these six years of my life with pleasure and appreciation for the children and teachers who let me be myself.

My first challenge, and one of the biggest ones of my life, came during the first week of school. The bell rang for recess, and we ran to the front door of the school. The asphalt playground lay at the bottom of the steps that began just outside the school. We ran down the steps and onto the playground. Kids at that age run in packs. They run for fun and to release the energy that they have built up sitting in the classroom. The group that I was a part of ran down the steps and across the asphalt. I ran with them. They split as they approached the slide, but I kept running in a straight line. The next thing I knew, I was flat on my back, and my nose was numb and hurting intensely.

I had run into the metal bar that braced the slide, squarely hitting it with my nose. I could feel the tears running down my cheeks in spite of my every effort not to cry. This was really a turning point in my life. I had lived on a farm, and I had not played with many children. This was my first time in the world beyond my home. Had I cried and continued lying there, it would have changed my life. A teacher would have come and picked me up. She would have comforted me, and the word would have gotten out that I could not play safely with the other children. But I did not cry, and I did not lie there. I got up and ran to catch up with the others. I could hear them yelling to one another, and I joined them. The most amazing thing happened. No one mentioned my accident. No child said a thing, nor did any teacher. I do not know if anyone saw me fall or if anyone cared; maybe they just accepted that someone had taken a fall. In any case, my right to play with the other children was not challenged.

I have often thought about how something so simple as getting back up actually changed my life. Hitting that metal pole really did hurt. I can still feel how my nose felt, but I never had a second thought. Lying on the ground was not a choice. The fun had passed on down the playground, and I wanted to be where the action was. If kids with disabilities are going to integrate successfully into inclusive settings, they need to be able to take a hard knock and keep playing. I got hurt a few times. In the fourth grade, I broke my collarbone playing tackle football on the playground; but other kids got hurt as well, and I was no different.

Within a few days, the academic work began. First, we learned the alphabet. My teacher had no experience teaching a blind child, and this was thirty years before public schools had special-education programs. So, my teacher and I were on our own. She got blocks with the letters on them in raised format. As she wrote a letter on the board or showed it on a flash card, I found it on a block. She taught us to sound out the letters, and then to link them in words. She would hold up a flash card with a word on it and spell it for me. I would sound it out and race the others to say the word. I used the blocks to spell out words, and then learned to write the letters on paper. While this method was slow when compared to the children who could read using their eyes, I developed a rudimentary knowledge of reading and writing.

I was learning, but it was clear that the method was slow, and using blocks would not allow me to read from books. The other children were beginning to read the first Dick and Jane book, but I had no access to the reader. Our teacher divided the class into three groups based on each child's reading ability. She put me in the slowest reading group. For the first and only time in my educational life, I needed my parents' advocacy. Had I remained in the lower track, school officials would have labeled me a slow learner. One thing would have led to another, and I doubt that I would have ever achieved the academic success that I did. If the expectations for me had been low, I would have never been pushed to do my best. I would have not competed with the other children. I would probably have never gone to college, found employment, or had an independent and productive life. Such a label can ruin the self-esteem of a child and confirm every stereotype about the incompetence of a blind person, but fortunately, my parents saved me from that fate.

I sat in the lower track for several weeks doing very little, until my teacher told my parents of my placement at a parent-teacher night. When my parents heard of my teacher's plan for me, they reacted with anger, forcing her to move me into the most advanced group. I heard very little about this confrontation. What I knew was that on one day I was in one group and on the next day I was in another. My teacher spent time with me, reading the workbooks and recording my answers to the work sheets. I sat in the reading groups listening to the others read and shared in answering questions about the content of the books that they read. Before very long, I had caught up in the workbooks and was a regular contributor to the discussions in the reading groups. I made the transition from slow learner to one of the top students in the class with hardly any difficulty. We just had to do things a little differently in my case.

Beginning with this transition, my teacher and the whole school adopted a way to teach me that became my way of working for most of the rest of my life. I had no way to read or write. The school lacked the resources to teach me Braille, and we were a half century away from the technological advances that make so much print materials available in electronic format. I listened in class as the teachers, and even more, my peers read to me. I have used face-to-face readers, and then later, recorded texts to learn and work. In my case, the school redefined what it meant to read. Reading meant understanding what was in a printed text, no matter how I got the information, and with this new insight, I excelled.

This approach worked for me. I learned to work math problems in my head. I imagined what the science diagrams and drawings looked like, and I learned to conceptualize maps and charts. I knew what was contained in those graphic teaching aids because I had to think them through. Attending school with sighted children was a wonderful experience for me. I developed a sense of myself that, while different in some ways from the others, defined me as a successful player in normal life. It is clear to me, however, that my success in this early experience in inclusion would not have worked for very many children. I had support at home, teachers who were willing to work with me, and peers who were willing to include me on my terms in their work and play. I was intelligent, emotionally stable, personally disciplined, well behaved, and cooperative. I would have benefited from having adaptive materials, such as raised line drawings, and I would especially have been aided by having Braille skills and materials. I did not learn Braille until I took a correspondence course during the summer of my junior year of high school, and then I did not really use it until I started my first job after finishing graduate school, when I was thirty-two years old. For children to be successful in an inclusive environment, they need adaptive skills and materials, and occasionally they need in-classroom and out-of-classroom support services. My experience worked well for me, but it is not a good model for others, especially in the current high-technology world in which they are coming of age.

My parents had little knowledge of educational methodologies. Neither of them was more than minimally educated. I do not know why they reacted so strongly to my teacher's placement of me in the slow group, but something seemed dreadfully wrong to them. They knew that I was not a slow learner, and somehow they realized what limiting the expectations assigned to me would mean for me, so they advocated for a change. They believed in my ability and me. Perhaps there is no greater gift that parents can give to their children than that constant faith that the child is valuable and competent. I recognize that my parents were not perfect, but I will always be grateful for their belief in me and their willingness to make that belief heard when I really needed it. It was their belief that a blind person could live normally and achieve according to his or her capacities that caused the school to change its policy toward me, and therefore, give me the chance to become an independent, productive person.

Throughout the next several years, my education proceeded smoothly. I took part in class activities and performed well, but the classes did not challenge me. This changed in the fifth grade. My teacher, Miss Mary Cottle, was a veteran educator, with a no-nonsense approach. She made her students do their work and correct any mistakes that they made. She posted lists of students who had spelling errors or who had mistakes on their math homework. One could not go out for recess until the students corrected their errors. Math problems were worked out on the blackboard, and she needed to certify that the student had done the problem correctly before his or her name could be crossed off her list and the student released for recess. When I made a mistake, she made me work the problem on the blackboard. She would read it to me and make sure that I could work it correctly. She made me write my spelling words on the board until she was convinced that I could spell the words correctly. She was a very stern teacher, but she challenged me, and I learned an enormous amount from her.

I developed a love for social studies in the fifth grade that has stayed with me throughout my life. Social studies in elementary school is a combination of history, geography, economics, and political science. Each day we read from our textbook and answered questions on a work sheet. Then our teacher quizzed us on the content of the assignment. I loved to answer the questions. She would ask a question, and I would raise my hand to answer. She would call on me occasionally, giving other children a chance to answer. A few of us would stand in the aisle by our desks, jumping up and down with our hands in the air, begging for a chance to answer. Often I could have answered every question that she asked. It gave me great pleasure to answer questions and participate in class discussion.

An occasional highlight of the social studies class came when we chose sides for a contest. When we chose sides for sports teams, I was always the last person chosen, but when the game was social studies, I was the first chosen, and almost all of the time, I was the captain of one of the teams, choosing those to be on my team. I knew the relative merits of the other children, and my team always won. That exercise gave me both enjoyment and self-confidence. I have always enjoyed being tested and participating in intellectual games. School did not always challenge me. Probably there were times when teachers let me off because I was blind, but Miss Cottle did not give me a free pass. She made me work, and I thrived with the challenge. The competitive challenges were also affirming. I am grateful that my teachers were willing to make me perform at a level of excellence. They did not accept that good performance from a blind child was good enough. At least Miss Cottle challenged me to do my best. After a year with her, I knew that I could compete with anyone. She taught me a lot more than math and spelling.

I loved sports, and the other children included me in the playground games. When we played softball, the pitcher would stand closer and throw the ball slowly. Sometimes, if the background was just right, I could catch a glimpse of the ball. At those times, I could make contact, and even on occasion hit the ball with authority. I could never catch the ball if it was hit or thrown in the air to me, but if the ball bounced along the ground, I could hear it, and I could catch it. I could throw the ball accurately if my target made a noise. Occasionally, when all the conditions were just right, I got a hit or made a play, and it made my day.

When we played football, I centered the ball, blocked, or rushed the passer. When we shot baskets, I listened for the ball to hit the rim, and then could shoot reasonably well. I did best at wrestling, but our school was too small to have a team and I did not have a chance to wrestle competitively until I reached college, where I became a starting member of the University of Missouri wrestling team.

It broke my heart that I could not play on the school sports teams. I loved baseball and dreamed of playing shortstop like Marty Marion, the St. Cardinal star player. I thought that I was a good enough athlete to play, but because I was blind, I could not play. It was important to learn that some things are not possible; one must learn to accept that reality.

However, one can compensate for his or her limitations. I compensated by listening to all the games on the radio and learning everything that I could about baseball. I knew the rules and the finer points of the game; I memorized all the players and their statistics. My friends kept collections of baseball cards. They would quiz me, and I took great pleasure in knowing all the information on their cards. To this day, I love the Cardinals, the University of Missouri sports teams, and sports in general.

In the sixth grade, I became close friends with a boy whose name was Billy Joe Moser. We were inseparable for the next several years. We worked in school together. He would read, and we would work the math and science problems, the language workbooks, and the social studies questions as a team. We stayed overnight at one another's homes, played other boys in two-man teams on the playground, and hung together in the halls. Bill was a wonderful friend. As we moved into junior high and the reading load got heavier, he was enormously important to me. I really did not have anyone else to help me with the reading. I owe him a great deal, but he was more than my reader; he was my friend, and we laughed and played, cut up in class, and caused minor problems for our teachers. He helped me be a normal, ratty, middle-school kid.

The week around Valentine's Day in 1954 was unseasonably warm. The spring-like weather seemed perfect for swimming, so we went to a nearby slough, stripped off our clothes, and dove in the water. February was not a good time to swim in Missouri, no matter what the air temperature was. We almost froze before we escaped from the water. We soaped the school windows on Halloween, and drank Bill's father's liquor out of his refrigerator. We talked in study hall and played ice hockey on a pond that we had been warned not to walk on. While our pranks were minor and our crimes only misdemeanors, I felt a sense of freedom and adventure from performing them. Even blind children cannot be well behaved all the time.

It is only as kids learn to assert themselves and have a will of their own that they learn to make proper judgments. These acts of self-assertion helped me to develop a will of my own. I cannot understate how important this is for a blind child, who is directed by others so much of the time. All too often adults feel that they must take special care to see that a blind child is not injured. All too often, a blind child spends all his or her time with adults and must do what adults tell him or her to do. There is too little time to get in trouble, and this is smothering to the development of a normal sense of self and a healthy ego. Well-meaning adults all too often instill fear of activity and of life into blind children. Fear cripples more than blindness. One must occasionally dive into icy water or soap a window to learn how to deal with normal fear. It is important to fear what can really hurt one, but it is devastating to live with free-floating fear that keeps one from living a full life.

In the fall of 1954, my father took the job of night marshal with the town of Troy. This changed our family in many ways. It was my father's first full-time job off the farm in his life. He was thirty-seven years old, and it was the beginning of his career in law enforcement. He worked for fourteen years with Troy, and then he took a job as a youth corrections officer with the state of Missouri. He stayed in this position until his death in 1983. We were, for the first time, economically secure, but I lost my reader. I also took over the everyday care of the livestock, feeding the hogs and cattle, milking the cow, and throwing down hay for the horses. I was at the age where I experienced my father's departure from the evening life of our family to be a huge blessing. I could be free to listen to what I wanted on the radio, go to bed when I wished, and work out with barbells in my bedroom. I deeply enjoyed the newfound freedom.

The additional family income allowed us to buy a bigger and better farm, where we moved two years later. During the last two years of high school, my brother, father, and I worked the farm. We increased our livestock holdings, planted much larger crops, and operated much more farm machinery. We cut wood and sawed it into stove lengths for the fire to warm our home, harvested corn and put up hay, and made molasses from sorghum cane. We all worked hard. My brother drove the farm equipment, and I cared for the livestock. I learned to scoop grain and buck bales of hay onto a wagon, wrestle a pig or a calf while my father vaccinated it, and throw a log onto a platform where it was sawed into firewood. The work was hard, but I loved to do it. It was exhilarating to feel my physical strength mature, and I enjoyed watching the animals grow. It was affirming to know that, even though I was blind, I was doing good and important work. The work that I did was equal to that of any sighted person who did the same tasks. I was strong and my work was good, and I knew it.

Not everything always went smoothly on our farm. One day soon after we had moved to the new place, when I got home from school, I found my father sitting at the kitchen table in a state of serious depression. During the afternoon, he had been plowing with the tractor, and it broke down. He was certain that it was beyond repair and our dream of farming was over. In addition, the fence was down at the wheat field, and the cattle were in the wheat. I said, "I will fix the fence." He told me to leave it alone, but I paid no attention. I went to the barn and got the tools that I needed to mend the fence and walked up to the field. I do not really know if I could have repaired the fence or not, but I accomplished what I needed to facilitate. I got my father up and working. He came up to the field and told me that he would take over. He told me to go take care of the cattle and milk, and he would fix the fence.

That night there was a talent show at the school. I was to make a speech, and my father and some of his friends were going to perform several songs. I happily went about my chores, practicing my speech to the cow as I milked her. I wanted to be good, because I believed that if I could make a good speech, it would help to cheer up my dad. I was right.

The audience warmly received my speech, my father enjoyed himself, and we got the tractor running. We never talked about this incident, but I believe it was a turning point in my relationship with my father. I had witnessed a time of weakness on his part, and I had asserted my leadership. I was still less a man than he, but we both knew that I was growing up. He quickly took control of the situation, but for a moment, I was the stronger. I think we both appreciated the moment, and for our own reasons understood that it was as things should be.

Adolescence is a difficult time for all young people, but it is especially difficult for blind kids. I have never talked with a blind person who enjoyed his or her teen years very much. It is a time when an individual must develop a sense of personal identity, grapple with career-related issues, and confront his or her sexuality and sexual identity. As do most adolescents, I struggled with all these areas of my growth.

During the ninth grade, my first year of high school, I enrolled in vocational agriculture. I met a teacher in that class who had a profound influence on me. His name was Jess Clontz. Mr. Clontz took an interest in me and helped me shape my career goals.

My father worried about what I might do with my life. He bought a farm with the idea in mind that I could make a life as a farmer. Enrolling in the vocational agriculture class supported his vision for me. I enjoyed our farming enterprise, but it was clear to me that I could not have a fulfilling life on the farm. I wanted an education and I life of ideas. I wanted to live in a larger world than our family farm would permit. I took the vocational agriculture classes throughout high school, but it was not farming that I learned. I competed in public speaking and parliamentary procedure. I have used these two skills more than any other thing that I learned in high school. They have been, along with typing, my most important practical skills that I developed as an adolescent.

I served as the chairman of the parliamentary procedure team and won praise for my leadership. It was not just what I learned that was important, however. Chairing the parliamentary procedure team gave me an accepted place among the other students. They looked to me to lead them in competition, and they recognized my knowledge. This activity helped me to develop a positive sense of self. I had always thought of myself as a smart kid, but the parliamentary procedure team helped me to solidify that identity.

One of the ironies of my high school years was that, while my father wanted me to become a farmer and applauded my participation in the vocational agriculture program, Mr. Clontz was directing me to activities that led me to a very different career path. He talked with me about college and what I might study, and on my first day at the University of Missouri, he came to campus and took me around to meet university personnel and helped me to register for my first semester classes. Another influence that Mr. Clontz had on me was one that he never expected. He had been a member of the wrestling team at the university when he was a student. I wanted to wrestle, and at my first opportunity, I enrolled in a wrestling class. Soon I met the assistant coach, Jim Little, who invited me to the team practice. I wrestled for three years, winning two letters and fulfilling a dream to be a competitive athlete. My mentor, Jess Clontz, pushed me to be a public person and an athlete. These were gifts of enormous importance to my personal and career development, and I owe him a deep debt of gratitude.

Perhaps the most important academic decision I ever made occurred between my freshman and sophomore years of high school. I was walking on our farm and thinking about school. The course schedule that I would take in the fall was on my mind that day. In those days, one was required to take seventeen solids over a four-year high school program. This allowed one to take four courses a year, have a study hall, and take physical education. Study hall seemed useless to me. I could not study because I had neither a reader nor materials in an adaptive format, so I faced a boring and wasted period. I decided, instead, to take another class. In the following years, I took geometry, chemistry, and physics instead of study hall. These courses put me on a track for college. While I had little opportunity to study and do all the work assigned in

39

these advanced math and science courses, I did well enough in them. On end-of-year national achievement tests, I scored at the eighty-third percentile in chemistry and at the ninetieth percentile in physics. I have often wished that I could have had the opportunity to study in these classes, not because I would have changed my career, but because I loved the subject matter and would have enjoyed understanding more than I do about their content. Still, I can read popular science books with understanding, and it gives me pleasure to do so.

I put off the decision about my future until my senior year of high school. I wanted to go to college and study to be a lawyer, but my father was frightened for me. He suggested that we talk with the town's optometrist. He argued that I should not go to college if Dr. Brockman said that it would be too hard. I agreed to the appointment, and not surprisingly, the doctor agreed with my father. College involved too much reading. It was not like high school. I would not be able to keep up, and it would be a very unpleasant failure if I persisted in my pursuit of a college education. I am sure that the doctor and my father had my best interests in their minds and hearts, but I paid no attention to them, even though I had made a halfhearted commitment to take Dr. Brockman's advice.

A short time later, college representatives came to my high school to talk with prospective students. I met with them and explained that I was blind, and I wondered if I could successfully attend their campuses. The representative from the University of Missouri said that he had heard of a blind student attending college, and if I were a good student and I wanted to go to college badly enough, I probably could be successful at the university.

I took his literature home and gave it to my mother. She helped me make out the application, although she had to struggle to read the forms, and I was accepted. The school superintendent, a very good man whose name was Claude Brown, contacted the State Rehabilitation for the Blind office and helped me to become a client of the agency. The Vocational Rehabilitation program paid for my college education, removing another severe barrier. No one knew for sure what a poor farm boy who was blind could do with his life, but it was clear that I was going to have a chance to find out for myself what fate had in store for me.

Without a doubt, the most stressful thing that I had to do during my high school years was to ask a girl for a date. Our Future Farmers of America (FFA) club held a dance each fall, called the Barn Warmin'. I agonized over asking someone to attend the dance with me. Finally, I got up the courage to ask a neighbor girl to go to the dance. To my surprise, she said yes. My friend Billy Moser and I double-dated. My father drove us in his police car. I think I performed adequately as a date, but it was a terribly uncomfortable event and I never again took a date to a dance during high school.

Dances are difficult for blind persons. Some young blind people who are less shy than I am enjoy dancing, but the thought of dancing nearly paralyzed me. There was too much ambient noise for me to find individual persons as they sat around the dance floor. My dancing ability was very limited. More importantly, I did not know how to talk with my date about my blindness. I was too self-conscious to say, "I'm blind, so I need your help." This would have made the evening enjoyable and I could have relaxed, but I thought such an admission would have horrified my date. The truth was that not talking with her probably horrified her more than any honest acknowledgment of my blindness could have. I suffered many years of agony before I learned that honesty is the best policy.

I was fortunate enough to have one girlfriend during my high school years, however. Diana Blakely was the granddaughter of a neighboring family. She lived in St. Louis and came to visit her grandparents during the summer. She was very attractive and outgoing. Undoubtedly she initiated our brief relationship. We went to a church ice-cream social, a couple of neighborhood parties, and a few family dinners. We exchanged birthday gifts and a few kisses. We also wrote to one another during the following school year, but I could not read her letters, so I never knew what she said to me. By the next summer, she had found a more responsive boyfriend, and I was heartbroken. Nevertheless, Diana was a valuable person in my life, and I am grateful to her for helping me to accept that if I could learn to be more open, I could find a woman who would love me.

I had many friends who were girls. We talked and did homework together, and I listened to their comments about other boys, but I lacked the self-confidence to move the relationship to a different level. When I was growing up, one of the important rites of passage for a boy was getting his driver's license. When my sixteenth birthday came and I could not get a license, I was forced to acknowledge that I was different from the others. My peers moved into a world of freedom and growing maturity that was not available to me. Their social lives expanded, and this included a more active relationship among the boys and girls as they began to think about more adult relationships. My already damaged self-confidence was completely shattered. I accepted that I would have to wait until I was in another environment before I could pursue a normal relationship with a young woman. I developed a dual personal identity during the last several years of my adolescence. On the one hand, I was intellectually precocious and cognitively mature, but on the other hand, I was socially immature. I repressed my emotional side. This is a bifurcation in my personality that even today I monitor.

In 1954, the United States Supreme Court handed down the *Brown v. Topeka Board of Education* ruling, which prohibited segregation in the nation's schools. At the time, the Troy School District practiced segregation; however, two years later, this all changed. African American students began attending the previously all-white schools in the fall of 1956. By and large, integration went smoothly, without any noticeable tension. To the best of my knowledge, there was only one incident. Two girls got into an argument in the restroom, and perhaps a little pushing occurred. There was some talk among the students, but in a day or two, they forgot the incident, and no other problems ever arose.

This incident led to one of my most embarrassing moments and one of my most important ethical lessons. The Sunday following the incident, my family went to Sunday school at our church. I was outside on the lawn talking with the other kids. The subject of the conflict between the two girls came up, and I said, "That's what happens when you put whites and niggers together." Janet Creech, a neighbor girl who was a year younger than I was, slapped me. She said, "You don't talk about my friends like that." I pushed her and she fell down, but she had won the battle with me, decisively. I have never been so ashamed of myself. I was trying to impress, but she called me on it, and I immediately regretted my bad behavior.

The culture in which I grew up was racist, but racism was not virulent. I am sure that the white people were insensitive and just plain ignorant of how their African American neighbors often felt, but they were not deliberately violent or mean-spirited. People in the community considered it bad form to use racial slurs in the presence of African Americans. Janet reminded me that I had stepped over the line. She went further when she called one of the African American girls her friend. My embarrassment taught me an ethical lesson that has stayed with me. I am truly grateful to her for teaching me not to try to gain from belittling another person. It was a valuable lesson.

A few years later, I learned more about the subtlety of race relationships in a small Missouri town. On Valentine's Day of my senior year, our English teacher gave us the assignment of making a valentine, writing a poem to go with it, and giving it to a classmate. One of the girls in the class was an attractive and talented African American girl. The teacher came to me in a secretive way and asked if I would mind receiving Rachel's valentine. Of course, after receiving Janet's lesson, I said that I would be delighted to receive a valentine from Rachel. I am sure that the valentine that I gave to her was of an inferior quality, far inferior to the one that she gave to me. I thought a great deal about the meaning of that transaction both then and since, and I think it was loaded with meaning.

While Troy was a liberal town for the time and place, interracial dating was still shocking. The exchange of valentines, although innocent in this context, still carried mild sexual connotations. My teacher chose the most neutral person, a blind male student, to receive the valentine of an African American girl. I am flattered that she thought that I would be pleased to receive a valentine from such a talented and charming young lady, but I am also a little offended that she thought that I was safe, in my opinion, because I was blind. Do I overreact? Perhaps, but I do not think so. This incident reveals a great deal about the way my teachers viewed race relations and blindness in the 1950s.

Less than three months later, the class took a standardized test that measured our mastery of English. I received 295 out of a possible 300 points. This was the highest score in the class and one of the highest that this veteran teacher had ever seen. She said to me with a touch of sadness in her voice, "Have you ever thought what you could have done if you had not been blind?"

Later, I relayed this incident in an essay published in a collection of writings on blindness. Someone who knew my teacher read the essay and took it to her. At the time, she was in her nineties. She wrote me a letter apologizing for the remark. She said that she did not want to hurt my life. She said, "At that time, people did not think about blind persons as they do now." The comment did not hurt me, but it did cause me to think. I was confident that I could have a successful life, but I wondered about what she thought life held for me.

One of the most disappointing experiences of my school years came near the end of my senior year. My social studies teacher informed us that our school could send a student to participate in a high school program in New York City sponsored by the United Nations. The teacher would choose the winner of a contest. Each contestant would write an essay, make a speech, and answer questions asked by the judges. I wanted to win the contest and go to the United Nations, but my social studies teacher, the person in charge of choosing the student who would participate in the program, told me that I could not compete. She said, "I just don't think you could go to New York by yourself." Other students who overheard our conversation told me that they thought that I would win, and I agreed with them. Later, I found that my father had asked the teacher to not let me compete. It was hard to swallow my disappointment, especially when I faced the reality that my teacher and my father did not believe that I could participate independently in the world that I so intensely wanted to join. Still, I had no choice. I put it behind me and went on.

By the end of my high school career, I had proven that I could compete with my sighted peers, but there were still many doubters. Many of my teachers supported me, but others, including my father, feared for my safety, but their fear had less focus. They did not know how I could make my way in the world, solve all the problems that I would encounter, and take care of myself. I certainly did not have all the answers, but I trusted that I would find a way.

CHAPTER 4

The College Years

O N THE COOL SEPTEMBER DAY that I left home to go to college,
I went about my chores as I always had. I fed the hogs and
cattle, milked and watered the livestock, and walked around
our farm for the last time as a working member of the family. My life
changed forever that day. We loaded up the car with my possessions,
a couple of suitcases of clothing, a radio, and a talking-book machine
from the Library of Congress talking-books program. The talking-
book machine was on loan from the National Library Service, but it
was my prize possession, because it gave me access to the library of
books, which I had discovered for the first time during the summer.
The library has given me enjoyment and an opportunity for learning
for the last fifty years. My father, mother, and little sister took me to
Columbia. They dropped me at my dormitory on the University of
Missouri campus, helped me carry my things to my room, and left me
to begin my new life.

Although I returned home to visit and even spent a summer on the
farm before my father sold it, I never had regular chores or helped on
any larger projects. I had been the person who did the everyday chores
that hold a farm together, and when I left, there was no one to do the
everyday feeding and watering, milking and tending. I have left other
homes and communities, and of course, other jobs, moving on to other
opportunities and adventures, but this move was by far the biggest of
my life, and it probably changed the lives of those I left behind more

than would happen ever again. My younger brother would briefly drop out of school and move to St. Louis to work in construction with our uncle. He returned home in a year, but a tractor accident severely injured him and the family sold the farm. My parents moved to town, making my mother's life much easier, and my father settled for a garden and a small barn, where he kept a horse and my sister's pony. When I went to college, the dream of the farm life ended, my family moved to town, and I began to look for a life. I was not sure what I could do, but I was not very worried about it. That was in the future, and in the meantime, I had some things to do. The future could wait.

In the fall of 1959, college dormitories were not gender integrated. Men lived on one side of campus and women on the other. The people I met that first day were all male. My roommate was like no one that I had ever met. He had a stereo system that he set up in our room, where he listened to jazz and classical records. He put a rug on the floor and papered the walls and ceiling with Playboy pinups. He was very cool, and I had no understanding of his music or even of the cultural models that he wished to emulate. He might as well have been from Mars. However, he was friendly and accepting. I must have seemed at least as strange to him as he did to me. I was blind, had few possessions, was perfectly happy with what I had, and desired only to go to class and find out about the wrestling team.

We did not become friends, but we were good roommates. We stayed out of one another's way and respected one another. His name was Jim Floyd, and a few years later, a car accident took his life. In a quiet and almost accidental way, I learned a great deal from him. He tried to be the sophisticated, hedonistic playboy. While I did not want to adopt this model, I appreciate what I learned about music and the larger culture. For someone such as I, who was looking for information about the world off the farm, Jim Floyd was an educational gift from the gods, and a good roommate to boot. Two years later, I met his brother, and we became friends. Dee Floyd became a major influence in my college experience. I can honestly say that the two Floyd brothers were among my most lasting educational influences during my college years.

During the first two years of college, the dormitory community provided me with my primary social life. Pat Scholes was my next-door neighbor. Pat and I and a few other boys went to movies together, played music, took our meals together at the large cafeteria that served the dormitory complex in which we lived, and on occasion took trips together to away football games. We played pranks on one another in the way of late adolescents, laughed a lot, and provided one another with the comfortable, supportive community that helped us to transition between our parents' home and our adult lives. Young men talk about many things—women, careers, past exploits—and occasionally we talked about my blindness, but not often. The boys in the dorm acknowledged that I was blind, but made very little of it. It was just who I was. Each of us had our unique qualities, and blindness was one of mine. The dorm community was accepting, supportive, and rather limited in its potential for personal growth. I outgrew it, but it gave me the transitional community that I needed to mature, make friends outside the dorm, and develop wider interests.

My first venture outside the dormitory community came when I walked onto the mat to try out for the wrestling team. In 1959, the university was rebuilding its wrestling program. The team had only limited resources and few scholarships. There were a number of Missouri high school state champions and runner-ups on the team, but it was not yet at the level of the top national programs. This meant that there was a greater opportunity for me. I was not exposed to high school or college wrestling. I knew nothing of the rules or the techniques of the sport, but I did know that it was a sport in which I could participate. I had heard that students at the Missouri School for the Blind competed in the state high school tournaments, and some of the boys did very well. I had always wanted to play sports, but I could not. I was not certain that I could compete with the experienced and talented athletes on the university team, but I was determined to give myself a chance. The years of hard farmwork had made me physically strong, I was in good condition, and I was determined.

In 1959, freshmen could not compete in varsity competition. This gave me a year to learn the sport. Coach Marshal Estep and assistant coach

Jim Little welcomed me on the mat and worked with me. The other wrestlers practiced with me, and soon I was a regular part of team practices. I came early and stayed late, hoping to make up for lost time, but it went slowly. As hard as I tried, the others were too much ahead, and I spent that first year getting beaten.

But I began to see improvement. I pinned one of my teammates in an exhibition match put on before a basketball game, and in a major breakthrough, I wrestled a practice match with a blind member of the team who had placed third in his senior year in the Missouri State Wrestling Tournament. He was an outstanding wrestler, who was also about twenty pounds heavier than I, but I held my own, and for the first time, I really felt that I was wrestling. When that first season ended, I felt that I was a member of the team. I talked with the coaches about my workout plans for the off-season and made plans for the upcoming year.

I wrestled both my sophomore and junior years of college, winning a varsity letter each year. I was not a great wrestler, but for a walk-on with no previous experience, I felt good about my performance. I had always wanted to be an athlete. I thought that I was good enough to compete, but I had never been able to play sports. It had been a major frustration throughout my high school years, but I accomplished that goal. I proved to myself that I could compete, and it removed a frustration from my life that set me free to do other, more meaningful things. Wrestling allowed me to be a normal person, even though I am blind. It provided me with an element of confidence in my ability to live successfully in the mainstream world. For this, I owe my coaches and teammates a serious debt of gratitude.

One evening toward the end of my freshman year, my roommate's older brother came by our room for a visit. Dee Floyd was an American studies major and a would-be intellectual. He was in the early sixties' gap between beatniks and hippies. If Jim wanted to be a cool playboy sophisticate, Dee wanted to be an alternative-culture dropout. He was very critical of all institutional structures—his father's cheese-making business, the university, any kind of political or governmental structures, and especially the family and religion. We quickly became friends. He taught me to play chess. He introduced me to his small circle of friends, and we would go out late at night for coffee and conversation about American literature, theater, and any other topic that we felt intellectually creditable. We attended plays on campus and went to St. Louis and Kansas City to see traveling productions of the serious drama of the time. We saw the Old Vick Company do Shakespeare and G. B. Shaw in Kansas City, and a production of *A Taste of Honey* in St. Louis. It was a marvelously educational experience.

Dee came by my room most nights to play chess. We would set up a chessboard under a lamp, and I would get as close to the board as I could. It took me a long time to play, because I had to understand each move. I could not see the whole board, and often I could not see the black pieces against the black squares on the chessboard. There are chess sets that are made for blind persons to use, but I did not know about them at that time. Dee was very patient. He never criticized me for playing slowly. He completely accepted my blindness, and on our trips offered whatever help I needed, but never tried to give me more assistance than I wanted. To this day, I think of him as one of my closest friends, although I have not seen or talked with him for forty-five years. He left the university after graduation to attend a graduate program at Florida State University in library science and then took a position with the Dallas public-library system. I have enjoyed close friendships throughout my life, beginning with Billy Mosier in middle school, and then Pat Scholes and Dee Floyd in my early years of college. These friends have accepted my blindness and me. They have enriched and educated me, and I owe them very much, indeed.

In the spring of 1960, students across the South initiated a revolution. They sat in at lunch counters, picketed restaurants that would not serve African Americans, and protested segregation wherever they found it. In the beginning, I was not very aware of these events, but by 1962, I was drawn into the movement. My route to the civil rights movement led through the Wesley Foundation, the Methodist college group. Pat

Scholes and I attended the Methodist Church while we were growing up. When we got to college, we went to the Wesley Foundation together. However, I stopped going after the first year. I felt that the group was superficial, and I never seemed to fit in. I considered the culture similar to a fraternity or sorority without the wild partying. But in the fall of 1962, Pat told me of changes at Wesley. A new campus minister, Bob Younts, had taken over the leadership of the group. Along with his assistant, Rev. Raymond Call, they were changing the purpose and program of the organization.

The new emphasis focused on a study of the new theology, social issues, and Christian action. He persuaded me to attend a few meetings and worship services just to see if I were interested in becoming involved. I agreed to do so, and that decision was to have a major influence on the rest of my life. Over the next two years, I would find a community where I would make a number of deep friendships, receive opportunities to become a leader, sharpen my writing skills, begin to date and meet my wife, initiate a life-long involvement in community action, and take my first steps toward defining my career. The two years that I spent with the Wesley Foundation group were truly a bridge to the rest of my life. It was at the Wesley Foundation that I began to feel and act as an adult. During those years, my blindness was truly a characteristic, not a disability.

In the early sixties, a wave of younger church leaders taught the neoorthodox theology of Paul Tillich and Reinhold Niebuhr. Drawn from the tumult of the national and international crises of the 1930s, the theologies of these thinkers attacked the liberal evangelicalism of the American church. They asserted that it was too bound to American culture, to corporate domination of workers, to patterns of racial discrimination, and to a shallow consumer-oriented lifestyle. It was silent on issues of social justice and chose to emphasize private violations of conventional morality over public ethical concerns.

The theology of Tillich talked of God as the "ground of being." This language helped me to get around the image of a God who was portrayed as an old man in the sky, a religious nonstarter for me, as it was for so many of my contemporaries. Niebuhr, on the other hand, was a strong advocate for social justice in a world filled with conflict and power politics. When taken together, Tillich and Niebuhr gave me a philosophy that was critical of American culture, helpful in avoiding narrow religiosity, and committed to social action. It gave me a way to affirm the American emphasis on equality and justice, the rightfulness of the critique of contemporary culture, and an institutional base and community in which I could locate myself. My personal identity was beginning to solidify. The critique of liberal theology and the institutional church seemed on target to a generation of students who saw the events of the civil rights movement on TV every night and who saw their religious leaders draw back from confronting the racism in their own congregations. Like so many others, I found a home with the movement.

During the 1962–63 school year, I developed a new set of friends. Jerry Boren was a central figure in this new group. Jerry was two years behind me in school, but was a few years older. He had joined the Marine Corps after high school and came to college when he finished his military service. Jerry was more mature, a curious student, and very sociable. We met at a Wesley Foundation retreat and quickly became close friends. That friendship has lasted almost fifty years. Jerry and a friend of his, Jim Hood, took me to meetings of students who were attempting to engage racial segregation and student apathy in Columbia. We joined groups of students that visited with the students at the Missouri School for the Deaf and inmates at the nearby state mental hospital. We went to Kansas City to engage in work projects and voter registration drives sponsored by the American Friends Service Committee. We went to St. Louis for work and training with the presbytery of the city, and I joined a sit-in organized by the Committee on Racial Equality (CORE). We were part of a group of students that published an underground magazine that we called *Catalyst*. We followed closely the struggles of the Kennedy administration as it became more active in supporting the civil rights movement. It was an exciting time, and we felt that we were a part of creating a new and better world.

Jim Hood's parents lived in Columbia, Missouri. He lived in an apartment in their basement, and during that winter, he invited first Jerry, and then me, to share the apartment with him. The apartment became the location for much planning and work on all our projects. It also was the location for my first real dating and relationships with women. Jim and Jerry had steady girlfriends, and I dated a girl whom I met in the community of social activists with which we were both involved. Julie Boone was a vivacious young woman who was aggressive enough to overcome my shyness and lack of confidence. We picnicked and attended parties, rode around in Jim's convertible on gorgeous spring days, and participated in social actions.

Julie and I dated for about six months before she found more interesting companions, but during that time, we shared soul-shaking events. The deepest of these was the assassination of President Kennedy. During the summer, I worked in St. Louis with a small Presbyterian Church doing community organizing. Julie went home to Kansas City, and we wrote almost every day. However, I could not read her letters and I was too embarrassed to ask anyone to read them to me, so I really do not have any idea what she wrote to me. I told her about my work and what I was reading. I discussed the news of the summer, including the March on Washington and Dr. King's "I Have a Dream" speech, but I do not know what she thought about any of it. I have often thought how disconnected those letters must have seemed to her.

We continued seeing one another through the fall, but by November, our romantic relationship had ended. However, we still enjoyed spending time together. I met her for lunch at the university library on November 22, 1963, and walked toward the Student Union. We heard the announcement over someone's portable radio that President Kennedy had been shot. I felt faint with the shock, and we sat down on some nearby steps. My room in a private rooming house was just a few blocks away, and we went there to listen to the reports. Both Julie and I had embraced the optimism of the past several months. We had moved from Kennedy doubters to uninhibited Kennedy admirers. It seemed to us that change was in the air and hope for a more just society was well-founded. As we sat in my tiny single room, listening to the discouraging reports and then to the announcement of the president's death, we felt all of that optimism and hope drain from us. We cried and did our best to comfort one another, but she needed to leave for a class, and we both recognized that we had deeper connections other places with other people. Still, no single event is more memorable to me from my college years than was the few hours that I spent with Julie Boone listening to and trying to make sense out of the tragedy of the assassination of the president.

As did so many others of our generation, we were forced to accept the terrible truth that one's best hopes and dreams could be crushed in a second, and there was no other choice but to pick up the pieces of one's life and continue. It was the end of a love affair with a woman and with a youthful innocence. Things were never quite so simple or easy after that, but in the days and weeks that followed, I took a major step toward adulthood. It is true that one's heart can break, one' dreams can prove unrealizable, one can lose one's way, and yet one can create new dreams, find other roads to take, and build new relationships. As long as one is alive, one must build anew. It is the central principle of a mature life. I learned its truth most intensely around the events of the Kennedy assassination, but I learn it over and over and hope I will never forget it.

During the summer of 1963, Jim joined his parents for a year in Algeria, Jerry married his steady girl, and I found a single room in a rundown old house the landlord rented to students. I had graduated in the spring; so when I returned to school in the fall, I started my first year of graduate school in the sociology department. During the previous year, when I lived with Jim and Jerry, I depended on Jim for transportation and on both Jerry and Jim for leadership in both our social and community-action activities. It was fortunate for me that our threesome broke up when it did. I had needed their help, but I now needed to be on my own. Living near the campus, I could walk to where I wanted to go, I could arrange my own schedule, and I could choose my own projects. I was ready to become a leader and excited about the opportunities. In the coming year, I would find my voice, organize a student volunteer project for the following summer, become a leader in several campus associations, and meet the woman who a year later would become my wife. I flourished in that beaten-up old rooming house.

The Wesley Foundation published a newsletter and a little magazine called *CRUX*. I wrote movie reviews for the newsletter and a series of articles for *CRUX*. My reviews primarily were of British and European films, and my articles dealt with the sociology of campus life. These were my first published pieces, and I felt great about writing them. I also chaired the education committee for the Wesley Foundation group. In this capacity, I directed a yearlong Sunday-night lecture series. I gave the first lecture, which provided me with the opportunity to set forth my position on the church as a social-change agent. I do not remember much of what I wrote or spoke, but I do remember well the satisfaction I drew from communicating with my audience. I definitely wanted my career to move in this direction. I was beginning to find a voice.

We planned a retreat for the Thanksgiving weekend. Our keynote speaker was to be Frank Littell, an American church historian from the Chicago Theological Seminary. He had written extensively about the role of religion in American society, and we were excited to have such a noted scholar with us. However, the assassination of President Kennedy occurred earlier in the week. When Julie and I parted, I went to the offices of the Wesley Foundation to find comfort and discuss whether to cancel our weekend retreat. We chose to hold the retreat as planned, believing that it would be helpful to our members to be together at such a traumatic time, and also that it was important for the church to engage such a tragedy and to contemplate what its role was in troubled times. We were but a small part of the church, but no matter how small we were, it was our part, and it was where our responsibilities lay. Everyone who had planned to come did attend. We were relieved that when the retreat was over, those who attended agreed that the event had been among the most meaningful of our lives. We knew that we could go on with our community involvement. If anything, we strengthened our commitment.

We were among the lucky ones who had a supportive community in which we could ground our optimism. We did not drop out or turn on. We continued our education, established our careers and families, and continued to work for what we believed would be a more just society. The Wesley Foundation community, at that time and in that place, gave me my most powerful experience of the healing influence of a religious community.

In the following week, I received an invitation to attend a national conference of student Christian leaders held on the University of Ohio campus in Athens, Ohio. I joined Fred Hudson, the chaplain and professor of religion at Stevens College, and two of his students in an auto trip to the conference. This began a working relationship that would last several years. Fred suggested that I consider organizing a student work project in Columbia for the coming summer. In January, he invited me to his home to meet one of his students. Her name was Melody Gibbons, and in October, we would marry. Fred asked me to lead a weekend work project in early February in the Columbia Housing Authority apartments, which involved his students. Then he invited me to be a coleader of Stevens students who would travel to New York City during the Easter break to do a work project with the Chambers Memorial Baptist Church in East Harlem. All of these projects challenged my organizing skills and leadership ability, but I thrived under the pressure. I would do similar work for the rest of my life.

Melody was a dance major at Stevens, but she was also interested in the religion courses that Fred taught. Fred had gotten her involved with a student project with one of the churches in the African American community. The week following our meeting at Fred's home, we took a group of students into an apartment to help a single mother of seven clean and fumigate. When we finished, I walked Melody back to her dorm and asked her if she would like to see a movie. She agreed, and our romance began. Melody had known a blind boy who was related to a friend of her family, so my blindness was not a completely new experience for her. We talked about it as our relationship grew, and she had little difficulty in making the adjustments that my blindness demanded. We fell in love as we worked in the community. She was one of the students who went to Harlem, and we conducted a door-to-door survey working as a team. In the summer she acted as codirector of the student project, and she worked with me on a number of Wesley Foundation programs. We shared a commitment to involvement and community action that bound us together. Melody was a person with a strong personality. She was talented, outspoken, uninhibited, and hardworking. She loved to teach, direct, and choreograph. Her friends trusted her and confided in her. I admired her energy and personal strengths. Our marriage lasted twenty-three years, and we are friends yet today.

During the spring break of 1964, I joined Fred and ten students in a work project in East Harlem. We met for several weeks before the trip to try to teach a little street knowledge. The summer before, I had worked in the inner city of St. Louis and had some experience with ways to travel safely in the city. Fred had lived and worked in Harlem for four years, while a graduate student at Columbia University. We were going to enter an African American and Latino community. Since the students were all young, middle-class, white women, the contrast between them and the community would be immediately recognizable. We were concerned for their safety and made a rule that no student could travel alone. Either Fred or I would be with them when they went out on the street. As it turned out, we broke into teams of two to do a door-to-door survey in the community, and volunteers from the church matched up with some of the students. We had no incidents, but looking back on the experience, I think it was about the last time that college officials would have approved such a project.

Our trip began with a flight from Columbia, Missouri to New York City. It was the first time I had ever flown, and as it happened, we flew through a rainstorm. The plane was propeller-driven and it did not fly as high as today's jets, so the ride was rough. I was one of the leaders so I needed to show confidence, but I felt anything but confident. That was probably the best acting performance of my life. However, all went well, and we landed in New York on schedule. The next ten days were an exciting adventure.

Mel Schoonover was the minister at Chambers Memorial Baptist Church. Rev. Schoonover was a wheelchair user. He was the first person with a physical disability with whom I worked. He welcomed us into the church and gave us our housing assignments. Some would live with host families in the neighborhood tenements, while others would stay in the nearby Ben Franklin public housing units. I stayed with a family in one of the high-rise public housing buildings. After going to the homes where we would be staying and meeting with our host families, we returned to the church for a thorough orientation. Rev. Schoonover lectured us on how to behave while walking on the streets, introduced us to the president of the East Harlem Triangle Association, a local community organization, gave an overview of the social mission of the church, and told about the project upon which we would spend much of our time. We would conduct a door-to-door survey in the neighborhood to collect data on housing, education, and employment. We would work in teams of two, and volunteers from the church would accompany student teams to guarantee safety. Later I used my training in sociology to process the data that we collected and to write a report summarizing our findings.

We immersed ourselves in the activities of Chambers Memorial Baptist Church. We attended a meeting of the East Harlem Triangle Association, where participants warned of the likelihood of strikes in the schools by parents seeking local control. On another night, the famous civil rights leader A. Phillip Randolph spoke about the growing potential for violent riots in Harlem and the other ghettos of the nation. We attended a party in an apartment in the public housing project, and one evening I led a group of seven students downtown to Greenwich Village to attend a play. This adventure confused the New Yorkers. They could not imagine why a single man would be escorting seven well-dressed young women around the city. We had several offers to purchase the time of one or another of the women, but fortunately, none of the students accepted. I achieved some credibility when I won a wrestling match with a community volunteer, but my most lasting memory of the week came on Easter Sunday.

We met with the Chambers congregation at the church early on Easter morning to walk to a nearby park for a sunrise service. As we walked, the congregation sang, accompanied by horns playing anthems of hope and victory. The sun was just coming up over the East River, and it seemed possible that even in the slums of East Harlem, a new and better life could come to pass. As we entered the park, a man stepped forward to speak with Rev. Schoonover. He was African American and appeared to be known by the minister. The man seemed confused, and I had a hard time understanding what he wanted. After listening to him for a few minutes, Rev. Schoonover instructed me to take the man back to the church and stay with him until the reverend returned. The man was a heroin addict who was withdrawing from the drug. He wanted to get clean, but needed help. The minister would take him to a rehabilitation facility a little later, but first, he needed to conduct the Easter service. He wanted me to stay with the man and not let him get away. For the next three hours, I kept this suffering man close enough that I could touch him at all times. He talked, drank glass after glass of water, played the piano, scratched his itching body, and poured out his sad life's story. I did not fear the man, but I feared that he would get away from me. If I let go of him, he could run, and I would not be able to catch him. Fortunately for me, and I hope for him, when Rev. Schoonover returned, the man was still with me at the church, and I turned him over to the minister.

When we got back to Columbia, I wrote a paper for a graduate class in history about my experiences in Harlem. My professor commented that my prediction of violence in the streets was overdramatic and unsubstantiated. That summer, street riots broke out in Harlem and Rochester, New York, touching off a pattern of urban rebellion that would last for the rest of the decade. My ten days in Harlem provided me with a powerful seminar in the realities of urban America. This would be my environment for most of the next ten years, and it was a major shaping influence on my life and career.

Mel Schoonover was living proof that a person with a disability could play an important role in a demanding neighborhood. He told me that his disability often made it easier for people in the community to trust him, and once he won their trust, he could win their respect and belief in his ability to help. I have found his insight to work for me. I have used my blindness as a tool to be less threatening. Given the societal attitudes about blindness, people who are often on the defensive and feel inadequate will feel more confident and in control when working with a blind person. One cannot allow these attitudes to structure a relationship, but they can open a door that might be otherwise locked. A person with a disability must be fully aware of his or her feelings to use a disability effectively, but one can do it.

Soon after we returned from Harlem, Melody and I and eight other students moved into the African American community in Columbia, where we conducted a summer program. We worked on organizing a tenants' union. Volunteers recruited residents of the city's public housing to attend a special city council meeting, held at the high school auditorium, to consider the passage of the first civil rights ordinance in Missouri. We operated a day camp for the area's children, conducted classes for children and adolescents at the Blind Boone Community Center, which is located in the city's public housing area, coached a softball team in a city recreation league, and generally won the acceptance of both the black and white communities for our project. I began organizing for the summer project shortly after Fred and I returned from the student conference in Athens, Ohio. I recruited the student volunteers, raised the funds for the programs, met with community members and local officials to explain what we would be doing, planned the activities, and found housing for the students. This was my first effort at community organizing. I knew few persons in the community in the beginning, but I made phone calls, introduced myself at meetings, went to people's offices, and took advice from Fred and other older and more experienced church and service leaders. I still consider this effort to be one of the more successful organizing projects of my life.

I had been able to walk to all my appointments during the organizing phase of the project, but we needed a car to operate the summer program. We needed to haul supplies, drive to the day camp, transport children, and run the myriad of errands that were a daily requirement of operating a program. Melody's parents gave her some money, and we scraped together enough from other sources to buy an old junker. It lasted the entire summer, although we needed to do some substantial repairs to keep it running. Melody drove the car for the project and registered it in her name. It proved to be an essential tool for our work and a valuable part of the group's social life. We would pile into the car for an impromptu picnic or to attend a movie. Melody and I used it to get away from the program for a short break, and it permitted us to handle a few emergencies.

Driving a car is an important part of the lifestyle of Americans, and this is especially important to males. At least in 1964, it was a serious role reversal for the female member of a couple to do the driving. Since I was blind, I could not drive. Driving was a sign of power and control. If I was to be the leader of the project, I had to deal with the issue of power and control, and the car was a central symbol. I could not order Melody to run an errand or drive me to a meeting. It would be bad for our relationship, and it was her car. I did not have the independence to go where I wanted, when I wanted. I needed to plan my trips, ask to be taken somewhere, show her respect, and whenever possible, use alternative modes of transportation. She had her own responsibilities, and she could not just exist to serve my needs. We began to learn that summer how to negotiate what I could expect her to help me do and what I needed to work out in other ways.

This complex issue is of the utmost importance to a couple that has a blind and a sighted member. It is hard for both persons, and the feelings of abandonment, exploitation, disrespect, and mutual confusion can run deep. It is a problem area without a permanent solution. There will be changes over time as each partner changes. The request for assistance presents problems. A couple cannot always separate disability-related requests from the normal tension over issues of dependency and individuality. However, when one of the partners is blind, blindness is always an issue. In the end, I believe that our marriage finally failed over these issues, but for the summer we worked out the use of the car, I learned to assume more of a facilitative role as a leader, and Melody found ways to balance her personal ambitions with the needs of the group and my needs as a blind man.

We were married in the fall, with all our friends around us. I finished my course work for my MA degree, and in January, we moved to Rochester, New York, where I enrolled in Colgate Rochester Divinity School. During the fall before we left, though, we had one last explosive event to which we responded. The working relationship between the Wesley Foundation director and students and the local Methodist minister had been very rocky for the past several years. Whether the minister was simply tired of Rev. Younts's challenges or some other precipitating cause emerged, we never knew, but he dismissed Bob Younts from the Wesley Foundation post. The students were hurt and angry, and we chose to demonstrate our feelings with a protest.

We stationed ourselves outside the church before the Sunday morning service and passed out flyers calling for the reinstatement of Rev. Younts and a larger church evaluation of the whole situation. Then, during the service, we took turns going forward to kneel at the altar in prayer for the broken church. The minister and the congregation were outraged because we so rudely interrupted their Sunday morning. The Wesley Foundation, as we had known it over the last several years, was emphatically terminated, and a curtain came down on an era. I had received a great deal from my association with the persons who made up the Wesley Foundation community, but it was clearly time to leave.

As I waited to board the flight that would take Melody and me to our new home and a new life in Rochester, I thought about my years in Columbia. I came as an adolescent. I had done farm chores the very morning that I arrived on campus. I had little experience with the world that I was entering, but things had turned out all right. I had made many friends, widened my cultural horizons, chosen a career path, and found a wife. When I came to Columbia, I was a boy. When I left, I was a man. Even though I was blind, I could work productively, lead others, and have my voice heard in the community. I learned to accommodate for my disability, and even use it to my benefit on occasion. I still had a lot to learn, but I felt confident about my ability to learn and grow. I looked forward to my coming adventure with excitement and belief in the future. It was hard to believe that so much had happened in five and one half years, but when you are young, life should be very full.

CHAPTER 5

Developing Academic Skills, Broadening Community Involvement, and Building a Family: The Rochester Years

WHEN MELODY AND I ARRIVED in Rochester, we had only the clothes we carried with us, a few boxes we shipped, and a few hundred dollars in cash. We had neither jobs nor any other source of income. We were expecting a child in May, but we were not worried. We were confident that we could work out the details and build our future. We were right to have the optimism of youth. We did work out all the details and create lives of rich friendships, academic success, community service, and career growth. However, during these years, we began to wrestle with the persistent issue of Melody's need to be an individual apart from me.

In January 1965, Rochester felt cold and dreary to two migrants from warmer climates. It was a northeastern city of over three hundred thousand inhabitants. The Kodak Company dominated the economic and political landscape, along with Xerox and a few other high-tech firms. Rochester experienced its initial growth after the War of 1812. Early industrialists built flour mills to process the wheat grown in the Genesee Valley. A few months earlier, during the summer of 1964, several days of rioting in the African American community traumatized the city. Leaders from both the black and white communities were working to address inequities in housing, education, and economic opportunities. Saul Alinsky, the well-known Chicago-based community organizer, had been called to form a community organization in the black wards of the city. It was, from my point of view, a very interesting place to be.

Colgate Rochester Divinity School (CRDS) sits on a hill in the southeast part of the city. In the spring, when the trees and flowers are in bloom, the campus is beautiful. Highland Park, the site of a lilac festival each May, lies just across Goodman Avenue. In the years while I attended, the student enrollment was a little below two hundred students. The environment was intimate. Students worked closely together. Families in the married-student apartments shared meals and babysitting. Often they would get together to visit or play cards. Many students found mentors in favorite faculty members. The school had enough resources to assist students to piece together the funds needed to live adequately. It was an ideal setting for a serious student to learn and explore his or her personal identity and professional goals.

The school was a seminary affiliated with the American Baptist Convention. Its primary goal was to prepare ministers and other church professionals for a denominational role, but many students found employment in other denominations and even in secular professions. CRDS was, in the middle sixties, entering into a time of ecumenical expansion. It was also enrolling a growing number of black students, who were demanding that the school place a greater emphasis on the black church and the religious experience of black Christians. The intellectual environment was diverse, open, and dynamic. Placed in a city undergoing large social changes, the seminary offered an exciting intellectual home. It was a microcosm of the larger American society. Eventually all of the major issues of the time made their way onto this small, idyllic campus.

Soon after I arrived, I met with a counselor with the New York Division of Vocational Rehabilitation to apply for financial assistance. I was familiar with the program from my experience in Missouri, where the agency had funded much of my education. I received some financial assistance, but by far the most important support that I received was information about the Recordings for the Blind (RFB) program. This information seriously changed my life. RFB provides recorded texts to students who are blind or dyslexic. The organization has a circulating library from which a student can borrow books, but it will also record books that are not already available. For the first time, I could have access to print materials at a competitive level with my sighted peers. The RFB Program focuses on the specialized needs of students unlike the Talking Books Program of the Library of Congress, which serves a more general readership.

For the first two months of our marriage in Missouri, Melody read my texts. When we moved to Rochester, she attended my classes the first semester and read the books for me. She was interested in the classes and even considered enrolling, but she had not finished her bachelor's degree and therefore could not become a student. At the end of the semester, she delivered our daughter and found that caring for an infant took more time and energy than she had estimated. She simply could not carry on with the responsibility of being my primary reader. The RFB discovery was of monumental value to us. With this new resource, I could study on my own and free her from the duty of reading my texts.

I could study as much as I wanted and do it whenever I wished. I could read more than just the minimum assignments. I could become a scholar. I had been an adequate student—good enough to get into graduate school, but not good enough to earn a doctorate. I made a vow that I would dedicate myself to becoming a serious student. I had not been able to commit to serious scholarship because I lacked the resources. I had followed other pursuits—wrestling and community involvement—but now I had no excuse. I felt some anxiety at the time. I was not sure that I could do the work and write a dissertation, which I would need to do if I were to earn a PhD degree, but that became my goal. I would not give up my involvement in community work or social issues, but I would become a serious student. That commitment brought me a great deal of enjoyment, and it has shaped my career to this day. Research, writing, and lecturing became a permanent part of my life.

I cannot be happy for very long if I am not involved in some form of serious intellectual pursuit. The RFB program is yet another element of my life for which I am truly grateful.

A few weeks after we arrived in Rochester, Malcolm X came to CRDS to lecture. Faculty, students, and members from the community filled the school's auditorium. Melody and I joined the African American students and other white students with involvement with the movement in the front row. Malcolm was dynamic. His message was disturbing to those white liberals among us. He said that we should stop trying to associate with our black colleagues and work in their organizations. We should, instead, go to the white suburbs with the message of racial equality. Our place was in the white community. He did not attack white liberals for being the devil in disguise, but rather for failing to take the hard but more heroic path of ministering to our own people. The black students applauded his admonitions, but the white students realized the difficulty of the road ahead if we took seriously his directions.

Malcolm X combined the black nationalism of the past with the black-power rhetoric that I had heard in Harlem the previous spring and a more conciliatory tone toward white people of goodwill. Blacks needed control of their own community, but whites had their own valuable role to play, working with white persons of wealth and power. On that cold Tuesday night in February 1965, we felt that new ground was being broken in the understanding of the possibilities for racial change. But five days later, Malcolm X was assassinated in a Harlem church. And, as in November 1963, a leader was gone, hope was lessened, and the realization that each of us had to carry the torch for social justice was sadly and painfully reinforced. There would be no savior!

During the late winter, the Johnson administration decided to escalate the war in Vietnam, beginning a tragic course that would wreck the Johnson presidency, cause inestimable damage to Vietnam, and deeply divide the American nation. This event also led me to an important relationship with the professor of social ethics at CRDS. Prentiss Pemberton was a man nearing the end of his career. He sought students who wanted to work with him and had a background in sociological theory and community involvement. I met the criteria, and he offered me an opportunity to become a junior colleague, which I gladly accepted. Over the next several years, I assisted in his classes and in his seminars with local church members, coauthored an article with him for a national publication, read his drafts of manuscripts of his theoretical work, and assisted him in his successful campaign to become a delegate to the 1968 Democratic Party Convention. I learned a great deal from Dr. Pemberton. He was an intellectual father, and I cherish my time working with him.

Dr. Pemberton was among the first outspoken critics of the new phase of the Vietnam War. He invited several of his students to help him organize a teach-in on the growing conflict. I took a minor role in preparing for this modest protest. We arranged speakers to appear who had expertise on the history of Southeast Asia, the insurgency in South Vietnam, and the difficulty in fighting a guerilla war. Dr. Pemberton raised questions about the justice of American involvement. A small group of peace-oriented persons attended, and the peace movement was underway in Rochester. Soon I joined demonstrations outside the offices of the local Congressman and committed to work against American involvement, a commitment that would last for the better part of the following decade.

In the winter and spring of 1965, CRDS became the center of a controversy that hit the major media. *Time* magazine and national network television ran feature stories on what became known as the death-of-God theology. William Hamilton, a dynamic professor at the school, was the major spokesman for the position. He argued that the movement of the last few centuries to make religion a private matter, and the abstract and intellectually inadequate natural theology of the eighteenth and nineteenth centuries, grounded as they were in an outmoded scientific understanding of the world, had severed God from the experience of ordinary people. God was dead to modern man. Hamilton was the lead theologian at the school, and it did not set well at an American Baptist seminary, which taught a doctrine of a living God, to have its top theologian professing by word and in print that God was dead. He was fired during the semester, and a few of his loyal students held a brief rally to protest the firing. I wrote a short paper decrying the violation of Professor Hamilton's freedom of speech, but the protest was very short-lived. It was the wrong issue at the wrong time.

The Vietnam War was heating up, and the civil rights movement was coming to its culmination. The best students wanted to engage these issues. We realized that it would not be possible to work and study at a seminary and proclaim the death of God, and we wanted to engage the pressing concerns of racial justice and war and peace. Our practical lives and our moral consciences combined to leave us little opportunity or even inclination to explore the meaning of the death-of-God theology. In the end, those who were in agreement with the theology of William Hamilton drifted away into secular pursuits, while those who disagreed had little reason to take an interest in a pattern of thought that contradicted the path of life that they had chosen.

In the spring of 1965, the central battleground of the civil rights movement was Selma, Alabama. The call came from Dr. King to gather in Selma for a march to the capitol in Montgomery. The call was heard on the CRDS campus. A meeting was held, where representatives were chosen and funds raised to pay for the travel. I desperately wanted to go. The cause was compelling. I did not want to say in future years that when the call came to join the movement on the barricades, I failed to answer. I volunteered to be a part of the group that would go south, but the other students refused to let me join them. They said it was dangerous and a blind person would be at more risk. They also said that I had a wife who was ready to give birth and I needed to be home. Although it was very painful, I had no choice but to accept their judgment.

As it turned out, the march was violent, but none of the CRDS students were injured. I did not want to acknowledge that I faced any greater danger than anyone else; I did have to accept that someone else might be exposed to more danger because he or she stayed to help me in a potentially violent situation. While I did not believe that I would create a dangerous situation for anyone else, I could not say that in a new, perhaps hostile, situation, I would not encounter obstacles that would slow me down. It was a hard and unpleasant confession to make to myself, but it was necessary if I was to accept staying home with grace and appreciation for the genuine concern that my friends had for me. I had to acknowledge that my blindness could present limits to my activities that I had to accept. It was an important lesson to absorb.

On May 3, 1965, our daughter, Angela Dawn (Angie) Page, was born. She was a beautiful, healthy baby, and she has been one of the true blessings of my life. In a few weeks, Melody would begin to dance again. She traveled to New York City several times to take classes, leaving Angie and me alone. I learned to care for Angie, change diapers, make formula, bathe her, and comfort her when she cried. Over the next fifteen years, until she got old enough to watch out for herself, I spent many days and nights caring for her. When she was six years old, I held her and told her that her grandfather had died. Over the years, we walked and talked together. Our relationship has gone through the normal ups and downs, but we have a closeness that is beyond what I often observe between other fathers and daughters. Angie is legally blind. This means that she has some usable vision, but she cannot read normal print or drive a car. I believe that her limited vision has given us a common experience that has helped us bond so deeply. She is a proud, competent, professional woman, and a loving wife and mother. Her two children are growing into successful young adults, and her husband, Scott, is a fine man. I point to my daughter with pride and gratitude. My blindness and her blindness have not interfered with our parenting, as it should not.

When that first semester ended, I had been engaged with issues of racial justice, the growing war in Vietnam, and serious theological controversy. I had found an intellectual mentor and established myself as a strong student. I had a new baby, and I needed a job for the summer. We found an announcement on a bulletin board for a job with the St. Simon Episcopal Church, a church with a largely black congregation located in Rochester's seventh ward. The seventh ward was one of two wards in the city with large black populations. I called and set up an interview. I took a bus across town and walked from the bus stop to the church. This was new territory, but I followed the instructions and arrived at the appointed time. The minister was waiting for me, and we had a very frank conversation.

Rev. St. Julian Simpkins was a cultivated man. He came from a solidly middle-class origin and served an upper-class congregation. He was the vice president of FIGHT, the community organization that Saul Alinsky's team helped to establish. He contrasted significantly with Franklin Florence, the president and third-ward minister of an evangelical church with a working-class congregation.

Rev. Simpkins asked all the obvious questions. What was my background? Did I think I could work with black kids? Then he got to the point. Did I think I would be safe, since I was both white and blind? I told him that sometimes my blindness was an advantage, because it made me less of a threat. However, I was a good negotiator with streetwise knowledge, and if all else failed, I was a varsity wrestler in college. As it turned out, all three of these strategies were required during the summer to handle one or another situation.

I am not sure that I removed all of Rev. Simpkins's doubts, but he gave me the job. The Johnson administration launched the Head Start program in the summer of 1965. Since Rochester had been a site of an urban riot the summer before, it was a target for the Office of Economic Opportunity's (OEO) programs. The St. Simon Church hosted a Head Start site that first summer, and I had the responsibility to work with the teens in the program. In following years, the program was directed at preschool children, but in that first summer, kids of all ages were included. I team taught arts and crafts class in the morning and led recreational and educational programs in the afternoons. We sponsored parties and dances on the weekends. On occasion, teenage boys challenged me, and my wrestling skills were an important asset. I was required to force teens wishing to disrupt our programs to leave. Seductive teenage girls tried to draw me into their sexy games, and older neighborhood boys competed for the loyalty of the teens.

At times the kids tried to take advantage of my blindness. I worked with about thirty kids that summer. I am not sure that I changed anyone's life, but we were able to maintain order, keep the interest of most of the youth throughout the entire summer, and avoid any serious vandalism at the church. I received ninety dollars a week, which paid our rent, bought food, and allowed us to care for our new infant. At the end of the summer, I felt a genuine sense of accomplishment. I had taken a difficult job and at least survived, supported my family, and begun my involvement in the city.

My blindness presented challenges, but I had overcome them. While some of the kids tried to take advantage of me, others wanted to help. I won their trust because I could protect them from disruptive individuals, but also because I asked them to help with the activities. I involved them in our planning, but did not let them stray into dangerous or inappropriate activities. Once on a swimming outing, one of the teens tried to hide in the locker room and drink beer that he had brought along on the trip. He wanted to involve another boy. I took another teen with me to the locker room to find and confront the disruptive kid. When I found him, I took away his beer and made him join the others. The boy and his friends threatened me, but I called their bluff, and nothing more came of the confrontation. The teen that helped me prevented the boy with the beer from hiding; he also was a witness to the encounter. My blindness was an asset in this situation. By involving the second teen, I called on his better instincts, and I had a witness. A potentially ugly situation got resolved without difficulty. It is also possible that my blindness gave the disruptive teen a way to join the group without losing face. After all, he did not want to hurt a blind man.

In the fall, I joined an ecumenical youth ministry. The alliance involved a Catholic parish, an American Baptist Church, and the Presbyterian Church to which I was assigned. Seminary students working with the three congregations formed the staff for the youth program. We conducted a street ministry, ran a coffeehouse in the basement of the Presbyterian Church, and took groups of kids on weekend retreats. The neighborhood in which we worked was ethnically mixed. There were white families from Appalachia, descendents from an earlier immigration from southern Italy, Puerto Ricans from New York City, and African Americans who had come north from Florida to work in the fruit harvests, only to stay in Rochester. We engaged the kids where we could and how we were able, but an incident at a high school basketball game gave us an opportunity to develop a program that may have actually made a difference.

My primary colleague was a fellow student at CRDS. Mike Losinger began the youth ministry program in the neighborhood. Mike was dedicated and talented. He was a man of genuine competence and a pleasure to work with. He had a strong relationship with a group of teens from the Italian community. One cold winter evening following a basketball game, these boys were leaving the game when they hassled a small African American teen. They knocked him down, but to their surprise, he came to his feet with a knife in his hand. He cut three of the boys rather seriously, causing them to be transported to a nearby hospital. Soon after the fight, Mike heard about it and went to the hospital to visit the injured boys. He called me, and I took on the responsibility of working with the boy with the knife. I met with his family, raised money for bail, and worked to have the charges against him dropped from a serious felony to a misdemeanor. Mike convinced the injured teens to acknowledge that they had responsibility for the fight and to drop their charges. The confrontation might have sparked further violence, but it didn't, and we believed that we had something to do with a more benign outcome.

Following the fight, we went to the three high schools in the area and asked the administration if we could work with them to promote increased racial understanding among their students. They readily agreed, and we created an organization of students trained to intervene in situations where racial conflict was potentially present. We had several meetings in the high schools, and then organized several weekend retreats for interracial groups of teens. These groups proved to be deeply moving for the students. We asked them to talk about their feelings toward other ethnic groups and facilitated the interchange. I led these groups and for the first time allowed my ability to listen to individuals in a group to make up for my inability to see their expressions and read their body language. I, of course, used Mike's input to confirm my own perceptions.

My experience in this situation and in many others leads me to believe that a sensitive and well-trained blind person has no disadvantage when working with a group if he or she listens effectively. A sigh, a movement in a chair, and especially the inflection in a speaker's voice provide the blind listener with information about the internal feelings of a participant that is as reliable as any visual cue. Feelings are expressions of the larger structure of meaning held by the participant, so understanding that structure provides a context for both verbal and nonverbal communication. A blind person is as able to engage a participant at that deeper level of meaning as is a sighted person, and I found that I had a talent for that level of engagement.

The weekend retreats produced a corps of students in each high school who were prepared to be peacemakers if trouble arose. We were gratified that no additional violence occurred. We never knew if our work contributed to that result. We hoped that it did, and the students said that their experience in the program improved their understanding of others; they were very happy that they were part of the process.

During the summer of 1966, I was invited to join a social worker with the public schools on a camping trip. We took a teen who had cerebral palsy with us in order to get to know him, and we hoped to gain some insight into what he might do productively after leaving school. This was a full decade before the Education of Handicapped Children's Act was adopted. I had little experience working with persons with disabilities, and while we had an enjoyable time with this youth, I doubt we discovered anything of worth for him. However, even though I did not know it at the time, this was the first experience of what would turn out to be my major life's work. It was a revealing comment on the state of services to persons with disabilities at the time that I would be asked to participate in such an enterprise. My only qualification for the effort was my blindness. Yet the idea of independence was in the air, and someone thought that perhaps a person with a disability who was living an independent life might have some positive influence on a youth who was also trying to become an independent person. I wish I had known more, but the experience caused me to think about how I might help others with disabilities. That thought would wait for eight more years to become a central force in my life, but that time would come.

During the 1965–66 school year, Melody and I heard again from our old friend from Columbia, Fred Hudson. Fred and his family had moved to Waterville, Maine, where Fred was chaplain and professor of religion at Colby College. He wanted us to take out a year and come to Colby to initiate a new program. He proposed that we live in a dormitory and work as resident hall counselors. I could teach and Melody could dance with the college company. Our daughter, who was a year old, would be an added benefit, since we would be even more of a regular young family if we had a child. After examining our misgivings, we accepted the offer, and in the fall moved into a dorm on the Colby campus for what would prove to be a very intense year.

Waterville is located in central Maine about twenty miles north of Augusta, the state capital. In 1966, its population was approximately twenty thousand. It was surrounded by cornfields and pumpkin patches. Small lakes and old farmhouses gave a rural flavor to the community. In the winter, snow covered the ground and piled up along the streets and roads. It was an isolated and self-contained community. The Colby campus set at the top of a long hill outside of the town, adding to the feeling of distance from the rest of the world. Most of the roughly two thousand students lived on campus, so our community was made up of a largely isolated group of late adolescents and young adults, who studied and played, fought and loved, and searched for personal and career identities among the snow-covered lakes and fields, the residential dormitories, and the classrooms of this upper New England educational enclave. It was our task to keep order, nurture, and challenge the young people in our dorm and on the campus, and we actually felt at home among our slightly younger charges.

We were responsible for two women's dorms that were connected. Approximately 250 young women lived in the two dormitories. In the past, single older women served as housemothers. A single room near the front entrance was an office, while another room across the lobby was a bedroom for the ladies. The bedroom became a nursery for our daughter, and with the installation of a couch bed, the office served as office by day and bedroom at night. I had another room on the other side of the building that I used for my office and study.

Melody handled the administrative work and counseled with the girls, while I assisted the students with academic questions and engaged them in discussions of social, political, and philosophical concerns. During the first semester, I assisted Fred in one of his classes and in the chaplain's program. I also coordinated the campus campaign for a peace candidate for Congress. We opened a coffeehouse in the basement of the chapel, and I organized a group of student volunteers to work with the local Office of Economic Opportunities. In addition to her work in the dormitories, Melody danced with the school company and cared for our daughter. Angie thrived in the dormitory. She had many ready babysitters and played enthusiastically with the students. It was a busy and rewarding semester, but just a taste of what was to come.

After the holiday break, Fred found that his PhD dissertation needed to be completed in the spring. His Columbia University dissertation committee decided to enforce the university's policy for terminating students who were not making progress toward the completion of their degree. Colby gave Fred a leave of absence to complete the dissertation, and I took over his work at the school. I had been approved to teach two classes of my own, and I took over a third class, which had been Fred's. In addition, I took over his duties as chaplain. I conducted all the programs with the exception of Sunday morning services. I also joined the local committee of Clergy and Laymen Concerned about the War in Vietnam. We participated in a march on Washington and spoke to church groups wanting to learn more about the opposition to the war.

One of my more enlightening experiences during the year came when I team taught a course on racial and cultural minorities with a woman from India. We compared Indian and American cultures with regard to the way in which the two cultures dealt with their racial and cultural minorities. Her family had been involved with Gandhi and the independence movement, but even so, she acknowledged that she still carried many of the old discriminatory attitudes. I shared my experiences working in the civil rights movement, only to find that my colleague opposed equality for African Americans. I also found that she had very negative attitudes toward persons with disabilities, especially blind persons. As it turned out, prejudice was not an exclusive quality of American culture.

As the differences emerged between us, the students had an opportunity to think about their own attitudes and values. While I did most of the work in the class, my colleague continually stated her concern that she would be left with the work. She did not believe that a blind person could teach sighted students at a college level, and she resented that she had been placed in such a position. Although we were pleasant to one another, our cultural differences were impossible to ignore. She came from a South Asian upper-class family, and I from an American rural working-class environment. My populism conflicted with her elitist mentality. Perhaps our students gained insight to the reasons why conflicts occur between persons and groups with differing cultural values. I hope that they did.

When the semester ended, my papers were graded, and the students were sent home, Melody and I packed our things and left for a summer of diverse projects. She went to Colorado to study in a Stevens College-sponsored dance camp, and I went back to Columbia to work on finishing my master's degree. Angie went to Houston to spend the summer with her grandparents. As we drove across the country, we listened to the reports on the Six Day War in the Middle East and tried to comprehend how much we had done during the past year. After my teaching experience, I knew that I wanted to earn a doctorate and teach at the college level. Melody wanted to pursue her dance career, and our daughter was developing happily and well. While the world seemed to be coming apart, we were whole and on our way toward lives of rich fulfillment and accomplishment. The contrast between the outer world of conflict and war and our inner world of promise appeared to us, as we traveled, to be impossible to reconcile, but it was a reality, no matter its incongruity. Our lives would not always be so full of adventure and happiness, but even in the most difficult times, I have puzzled over this mismatch between my private world and the tumultuous public reality.

After a summer apart, we gathered back together for the beginning of the fall semester at CRDS. Angie had broken into speech during the summer. Melody was inspired to form a dance company in Rochester, and I wanted to settle down to a year of serious study. After years of intense community involvement, I was ready to dedicate my time and attention to academic pursuits. I needed to prepare myself for the rigors of a demanding doctoral program, and this was the year to do it. While this was my goal, and in truth, I largely fulfilled my commitment, events pulled me into the larger community. In many ways, the 1967–68 school year was the most focused year of my life.

However, two powerful forces were at work in American society during this year, and they were active in the CRDS community as well. The coming year of 1968 was an election year, and the war in Vietnam was dominating the political debate. In January, Prentiss Pemberton and I published an article in the *Christian Century*, a widely read national weekly, calling for protesters to turn their opposition into political action. A few days after our article was published, the Viet Kong and North Vietnamese launched the Tet Offensive, changing forever the course of the war. Eugene McCarthy challenged President Johnson for the Democratic Party nomination, and Dr. Pemberton ran for and won a position as a McCarthy delegate to the national convention.

The second force bringing change in 1968 was the rise of the black-power movement. During the 1967–68 school year, the movement on campus generated the creation of a dialogue between the black students and the white administration, which was facilitated by a series of leaders from the black community. Best known of these leaders was a young Jessie Jackson. I participated in these seminars and discussions, listening and trying to grasp what might be the role of a white student in the new direction that the civil rights movement was taking. The words of Malcolm X were on everyone's minds during these sessions. The black students wanted representation on the board of directors of the school, in the administration and faculty, and in a larger number of African Americans in the student body. In the following year, black students would seize the central building on campus and lock out faculty, white students, and administrative personnel. In the end, many of their demands were granted.

In March, President Johnson announced that he would not seek reelection, much to my relief. Then a few weeks later, on April 5, Martin Luther King Jr. was murdered, and once more, much of the nation and I were plunged into mourning. On a campus as sensitive to racial issues as was CRDS, the assassination of Dr. King came as a particularly hard blow. Many of us simply wanted the year to end, so we could recover from the storms of controversies and grief, but that was not to be.

At the beginning of the summer, Melody and I returned to Columbia so that I could finish work on my MA degree. I planned to finish my degree during the summer and return to Rochester for my last semester. I looked forward to joining the Kennedy campaign and helping to elect a man who promised to end the war and bring hope back to the national psyche. Once again, the hope was snuffed out by an assassin's bullet. A summer that was to be one of rest and recovery in an atmosphere of hope and promise became a grind to complete my degree and a struggle to fight off despair.

I received my degree at the August graduation and received an even more important confirmation of my growing academic ability when the sociology department offered me a scholarship to return for doctoral-level work. I wanted to attend the University of Chicago, so I declined the offer, but it meant a great deal to me. My commitment to an academic career appeared to be bearing fruit.

Even though the world seemed to be falling apart, my career was on track, and my family life was happy. As we returned to Rochester, we passed through Chicago, where the police were rioting and peace activists were being beaten. I felt both guilt for not being there and dismay that, while so much disruption was occurring, our lives were moving forward pleasantly and successfully.

When we arrived back on campus at CRDS, we were forced to do an analysis of our finances, and we determined that Melody would need to find a job. She worked rather steadily outside our home for the next six years, while I finished my education. In the fall of 1968, she found a position at a nearby institution that housed patients with affective disorders. She worked with a team that conducted recreational therapy activities. She led therapeutic dance classes and for a time thought of making this a career focus, but soon gave up the idea. The real significance of this job did not become clear until years later. She needed a career apart from my work that could allow her to express her own creativity and individuality. While I earned praise for my academic and community work, she lived in my shadow, or at least that was how she felt. This was a current in our relationship for the next two decades, until we finally divorced in 1987.

I benefited from her assistance in many ways. It was convenient to use her as a reader or driver. She ran all the errands, paid the bills, drove our daughter to day care, and generally facilitated my work. I received credit for whatever I accomplished, and she was complimented for being such a fine person for supporting her blind husband. I was too ambitious and determined to prove to the world that I could succeed in life even if I were blind to really understand what was happening. We loved and respected one another, but we were too young and inexperienced to handle all of the issues, and at that time, we were not even conscious of what they were.

I finished my class work during the fall semester, and we moved off campus while I waited to find out what graduate schools would accept my applications. I took a position as an interim pastor at a small church in a transition neighborhood and initiated a personal reading program aimed at preparing for graduate school in the fall. Melody wanted us to move to Boston, but I dreamed of the University of Chicago. She believed that there would be many more opportunities for her to dance in the Boston area than in Chicago, so I agreed that if I were accepted at Harvard, we would go to Boston.

It came as a major disappointment when my letter from Harvard came refusing to accept me as a student into the ethics program. The letter was clear. While I was a well-qualified student, the admissions committee felt that a blind person could not do the enormous amount of reading required to complete a doctorate in their program. While in a decade there would be nondiscrimination legislation covering this type of situation, at the time, I had no recourse. I was accepted by Boston University, but forced to choose between the University of Chicago and Boston University, I chose Chicago, even though it was a city to which Melody was bitterly opposed. She accepted my choice with grace, if not with enthusiasm, but I have often wondered what difference it might have made if we had moved to Boston.

The church that I served was associated with the United Church of Christ denomination. Its membership was primarily older persons who had attended the church for most of their lives. Their children had grown up and moved to the suburbs, taking the life and youthful energy of the church with them. The neighborhood was largely populated with newly arrived African American families. The members of the church felt alienated from the surrounding neighborhood, although once they had felt at home in it. They were fighting to save their church and community, but they had little hope of either happening. My job was to be a caretaker for the few months between finishing my class work at CRDS and moving away to begin graduate school. I did what I could, but I was young and optimistic and they were old and discouraged. I wish that I would have done more, but all that I really did was to get them through a few more months while they waited for the end to come.

We left Rochester in early September 1969 and trekked to Chicago. We had become adults during the years in Rochester. We had a child. Both Melody and I had done valuable work. I had become a serious student, received two master's-level degrees, and engaged deeply the more important issues of the time. I had found new resources to use in my studies, and I had begun to define my career. I had proven that I could perform well in a variety of settings, even though I am blind, and I had a more mature grasp of my strengths and limitations as a blind person. There had been joy and pain, success and disappointment, personal growth and personal failure, but the curve was rising, and the future looked bright. As we left Rochester for the last time, I felt a sense of pride and accomplishment. I was ready for the next challenge.

CHAPTER 6

The Chicago Years: Study, Personal Crisis, and the Realities of Blindness

I N SEPTEMBER 1969, WHEN WE arrived in Chicago, the city had the feel of a late industrial giant. It was large, dirty, and dangerous. During the four years we were in the city, Melody was robbed at gunpoint in the entryway to our building, three persons were murdered in the park outside our apartment, and a man resisting a robbery was shot and killed in our block. Memories of the 1968 Democratic Party convention were fresh in everyone's minds, and no one, especially a woman, felt safe out after dark. Suet from the burning of soft coal, which provided much of the city's energy needs, coated everything inside and out and left a taste in the mouths of the residents. As the 1960s ended, the memories of four assassinations, a deadly and unpopular war, and racial conflict and violence filled the hearts and minds of the nation's citizens. Chicago seemed to us to embody America, and it was very tough, indeed. If Rochester and CRDS had seemed idyllic, Chicago and the university seemed impersonal, cold, and threatening. We were going to be tested and stretched, but as the saying goes, "What doesn't kill you makes you stronger."

We lived in married student housing on the northern border of Hyde Park, the University of Chicago community. It was an island in the huge South Chicago ghetto. On the first day after we arrived, Melody went out to shop and got lost. She drove around the south side of

Chicago for several hours, and when she finally found her way back to our apartment, she was frightened and highly skeptical of the wisdom of our move to the city. While in Rochester we lived in furnished apartments, so we owned very little furniture or household goods. We had purchased furniture in Rochester and arranged for it to be delivered to our Chicago address, but the order was lost, and it was several months before we had furniture. We were not off to a very good start in our new home. However, gradually we found our way around the city. Our furniture came, we got a kitten, and we made friends. We found a preschool for Angie and started to learn to live in urban America.

The university drew me to the city. Soon I enrolled and began classes. The University of Chicago is a great university, and it was everything that I had hoped it would be. I found out that I had been very fortunate to be admitted. The year before, the faculty in my program made the decision not to admit anyone for the upcoming year. This decision was based both on financial considerations and student-faculty ratios, but the students in the program protested the decision and the faculty relented. Three students were admitted. One was a Catholic priest with a Caribbean background. The second was a young African American minister, and I was the third. For the next four years, I experienced the best in higher education that the world has to offer. I worked with internationally known scholars, brilliant peers, and a supportive administration. I deeply appreciate my years at the University. They prepared me well for my multifaceted career that would follow.

I enrolled in the Ethics and Society program in the Divinity School. This program sought to train scholars to study the relationship among human values, social science, and political power in the formation of public policy. The concern was not for abstract formulae for personal behavior. It was, rather, a pursuit of public-policy options grounded in examined values, relevant information, and practical realities. This approach to the ethical life calls for action in a diverse world. One must know the facts of an issue, understand the interests and power constellations, and at the same time have the philosophical grounding to act with ethical purpose. It is an ethic of a democratic society. It contemplates compromise, relativity, and limited goals, but it always calls for a clear value perspective. This perspective flows from the American tradition of pragmatism, but with a serious attempt to answer the critics who view this perspective to be so relativistic that it has no anchor in values. I have tried to base my life in this ethical perspective as I have engaged in personal and public action. I believe this perspective offers credibility in the dangerous and unpredictable world to come.

Each student is challenged to develop his or her values in a clear and coherent philosophical position. This statement, then, becomes a foundation from which to evaluate and formulate public-policy alternatives. This is undoubtedly the most difficult part of the program, but I found it to be of lasting importance. I began by asking the question "What does it mean to be fully human?" Drawing from the work of Martin Heidegger, I concluded that to be fully alive and human means to care for others and for the natural world, and to tend to their well-being. Drawing from Erick Erickson, I moved further to state that to care requires both freedom and a sense of responsibility. Only those with a strong self-identity have the personal power to effectively care; only those who are free can be truly responsible. One must have personal autonomy, the capacity for self-initiation, competence, and ego strength to be free, but one must also have fundamental trust, the ability to make commitments, establish intimacy with others, and possess the desire to care for and tend to the adult structures of one's life, family, public institutions, and the next generation to be responsible. Each person, as he or she moves through the life cycle, is called upon to master the necessary developmental tasks to become fully human. Each individual and social institution must nurture the individual so that he or she can become a free and responsible fully developed person. Each of our institutions and policies can be evaluated according to its success in contributing to the creation of a free and responsible social order. While this formulation did not answer all the questions, it did give me a foundation from which to work as I did my research, and later as I attempted to function as a policy maker in the real world of education and politics.

During the four years that I studied at the University of Chicago, I took classes with outstanding faculty. My major advisor was Gibson Winter, who introduced me to the German philosopher Martin Heidegger. I studied with the well-known historian of American religion Martin Marty, and with the sociologist of education Robert Dreeben. Donald Browning introduced me to the work of Erick Erickson, and Warner Wick taught me to appreciate the ethics of Aristotle. Benjamin Nelson led me to engage the work of the German sociologist Max Weber, and included me in a group of students who explored informally the science of culture and civilization. Every class I took was challenging, and I believe the educational experience provided to me by the men and women at the University of Chicago is second to none. During my third year, I settled on the topic of educational reform for my dissertation research. The university has a tradition of concern with educational reform that goes back to the work of John Dewey in the 1890s. It was a privilege to work with scholars in that tradition.

As an undergraduate at the University of Missouri, I considered for a time becoming a secondary education teacher. I took education classes and earned a temporary teaching certificate from the state of Missouri. My interest in education became reinvigorated when my daughter entered kindergarten. She attended Shoesmith Elementary School, a nearby neighborhood public school. I volunteered at Shoesmith, and when the Chicago School Board made an effort to decentralize, I ran for the Shoesmith neighborhood council and was elected. Later I became a Shoesmith representative to the regional council. While these positions had little power and I had little time to really engage the Chicago educational bureaucracy, I did get a better view of the massive problems faced by urban educational programs. This practical involvement tempered my hope for reform. Americans look to education to solve the social problems that exist in the life of the nation. They also expect the educational system to prepare their children for a better life than they have. These are impossible expectations and they place impossible pressures on the schools, but these expectations and the reforms that they generate also give the student a fertile field to study in order to understand the competing visions of the future that battle for the control of American culture. I studied educational reform because I wanted to understand the diversity in American life and the conflicting visions for the future that are loose in our culture.

I identified four perspectives on reform that even today seem to loosely define the cultural struggles going on in American life. A functional bureaucracy exists to ensure that all citizens are fed, clothed, housed, educated, and cared for throughout life. Then, we have radical individualists who want the bureaucracy to go away so that they can be free to follow their own purposes without the burden of others. Another vision is grounded in the unique values of a group or religious faith and seeks to convert the whole of the culture to its way of thinking. Finally, another perspective calls for a return to responsible living on spaceship earth. This last group seeks balanced consumption among the world's peoples; an appreciation for the damage human technology is doing to the land, air, and water; and for much more attention to be paid to the value of all persons around the world, especially women and children. It should be obvious that I identify with the fourth of these perspectives. While each of them is seriously held by their advocates, I concluded long ago that only the fourth provides the balance and restraint needed for each of us to have an opportunity to be free, responsible, and fully human.

One must absorb a great deal of information to work through a doctoral program at a major university. The Harvard Admissions Committee clearly told me that a blind person simply couldn't compete. Of course, they were wrong. By 1969, when I began my program at the University of Chicago, the Recordings for the Blind program was well developed. It was an essential part of my education. The Princeton, New Jersey–based organization held a circulating library that was made up of all the volumes that its volunteers had recorded. Many of the books that I needed were contained in this library, but a large number were not. Fortunately for me, a branch studio of RFB was housed on the university campus. For the four years of my residency at the University of Chicago, the dedicated volunteers of RFB recorded a continuous stream of books that in a concrete way made my education possible. A volunteer sat in a booth and read into a recorder, while another person monitored the reader to catch errors. The final product was a book recorded on reel-to-reel tapes. A master was kept and sent to the central library for future use by other blind students.

Truly this group of anonymous persons contributed to my life in a way that they probably did not completely grasp, but I know what a tremendous gift they gave to me, and I have been grateful to them for more than I was ever able to tell them. No matter how independent and self-sufficient a blind person wishes to be, he or she must acknowledge how important the support of others is to his or her success. I recognize how much I owe to the assistance of others. I do not believe that this takes away from my own hard work and achievements, but I believe that it does make me more sensitive to just how interdependent we all are. One's achievements require humility and generosity toward others. Only in this way can we strengthen the bond with each other.

My studies at the university proceeded without a hitch. I completed the required class work, prepared research papers, and took the orals that qualified me for writing a dissertation. I developed a dissertation proposal that was accepted by my faculty committee, and I completed the language requirements. My work was rewarded with a Divinity School scholarship. At the end of the fourth year, I was ready to leave Chicago with all but the dissertation completed for the doctoral degree. It had been a successful educational experience and I was very happy with my progress, but my personal life had not been so successful. My marriage went through a deep crisis, which shocked me to the core of my sense of self-worth. In retrospect, I understand better how my insecurity, primarily as a blind man, placed strains on our relationship that were very difficult for Melody, but at the time I could barely get through the pain and embarrassment.

During the second year that we were in Chicago, the pressures that were building up in our marriage came to a head. Melody took a job on campus and looked for a dance company, but she was not able to find a place to perform. Her dreams for a professional dance career were proving to be unobtainable, and she was deeply unhappy. She did not like the city. She felt that she was sacrificing her career for mine, and she felt that I was not giving her the affirmation that she wanted from a spouse. She could have gone back to school to finish her education, but she felt that we did not have the financial resources to permit both of us to be in school. She felt trapped, angry, and very unhappy. Unfortunately, we lacked the awareness and maturity to openly confront our situation.

I, on the other hand, was enjoying my studies; I was completely engaged in a very demanding program. I could not understand why she did not make the commitment to return to school. I was more than willing to take out loans and live very modestly. I wanted her just to make a decision about where she wanted to study and get on with it. I told her that I believed in her intelligence and ability, and I could not understand what she meant when she said that I did not give her the support that she needed. She needed help and support and reassurance that her career was as important as mine. I did not know how to give her what she so desperately wanted. I could not imagine quitting school nor could I understand how I could make the situation any better, so we floated for several months.

During the following summer, a friend of Melody's from her work told her about a weekend retreat, where participants would have the opportunity to join in group activities aimed at addressing personal issues. I hoped that she would find some direction from participating in the weekend encounter group. In the fall, she took a Spanish class sponsored by a community education program. I felt that this was a good development. She was getting out and finding things of interest to her that might give her a sense of having things to do that were not associated with me. As time went on, she spent more and more time with a Spanish-speaking tutor in her class. A few months later, she told me that she would like a separation. She and the man with whom she was studying wanted to live together. She told me that she wanted to have an affair with life. She moved out of our apartment and took our daughter with her.

I was devastated and physically ill. I could not study or even attend classes. I had always been able to handle life, but this was completely beyond my control. It exposed all my self-doubts and insecurities. I had depended on Melody for many aspects of daily living, such as shopping, cooking, cleaning, matching my clothes, and often for transportation. I wondered how I could do these simple tasks without her. At a deeper level, I wondered if anyone would ever love me, if my blindness would be a barrier to ever having a successful relationship. I had always been a successful person. This was failure, and I was embarrassed to talk with anyone about it. I felt rejected, and it brought out my deepest insecurities. I was completely confident that I could perform as a student or professional person, but I doubted that I could give a woman what she needed. I wondered if I could, as a blind man, be an adequate husband. I could not talk with my parents, and I never did tell them about our separation. I felt alone and empty, and I did not know how to pick up the pieces of my life and start over again. I learned, as time went on, that the issues that I faced were not entirely related to my blindness. Many of them were the same issues that many, many couples face; however, at the time, it seemed like the practical and emotional issues that I faced were deeply rooted in my blindness.

During the first few weeks after Melody left, I told no one. I picked up a few items from a local grocery store and managed to stay alive. I had never lived alone in an apartment before, so I had little experience with performing the basic tasks of daily living, but gradually I began to realize that I needed to rise to the challenge of looking after myself. I experimented with preparing simple, nutritious food, took a sponge and a bucket and cleaned the floors and bathroom, and for the first time I used Braille to identify papers, canned food, and boxed items. I taught myself to use a cane to travel independently, and I found a reader to help with mail and shopping. While I was still very unhappy, I began to appreciate my capacity to live independently. I felt much less depressed as my basic strong sense of self-confidence resurfaced. I was starting to live independently as a blind person, and it felt good. I took my daughter for overnights and on alternating weekends. I cooked for her, washed her clothes, and took her with me on walks in the neighborhood. My time with Angie added to my confidence. I began to believe that I would reclaim my life.

During February, two women acquaintances invited me to go skiing with them. They knew one another from work at the university and knew that I was having a hard time. We drove to Minneapolis, where we stayed in the home of Eileen's parents. The drive was memorable, because we drove into a blizzard. We were forced to stop frequently to knock the snow out of the wheel wells. Finally we gave up and spent the night in a motel. The trip through the blizzard brought us closer together, and in later years, Jo Ann and I would attend Chicago Cubs' baseball games together. However, over the weekend, I felt a growing bond with Eileen. I had never skied before, but I enjoyed practicing on the beginner slope. The combination of outdoor exercise and the fun of learning a new sport, along with forming new friendships, especially with Eileen, boosted my spirit immensely.

When we returned to Chicago, I invited Eileen to have dinner with me. She accepted, and we began to date. Soon we were seeing one another every evening, and we developed a deep and loving relationship. We shared a great deal. However, most important, she was not threatened by my blindness. She liked art, and we went to the Chicago Art Museum, where she described modern art masterpieces. She liked to read, and she shared some of her favorite books. She also challenged me. I was having difficulty with school, so she pushed me to take off a year and find a job. She expected me to be a normal man, travel independently throughout the city, find regular employment, and give her the time and attention that she needed. She was not threatened by my career; rather, she encouraged me to pursue my goals. She wanted a home, children, and a husband who could help her make that dream come true, and she wanted me to share that dream with her. I was flattered and invigorated by her love, and we almost made it work.

In the spring, Melody approached me about seeing a marriage counselor. I agreed, and in our first session, she told me that she would like to reconcile. Her request threw me into emotional turmoil. On the one hand, I had pulled myself back together and was prepared to move on with my life, but on the other, I could return to my marriage, have my daughter in my life again, and get on with my graduate program. I could avoid the embarrassment of a divorce and hope that everything would work out. I felt that Eileen had given me so much as I tried to recover from the crisis of the winter, but I also believed that a marriage should be saved, if possible. I was a student of ethics, and I struggled to understand the right thing to do. I understood that the easy thing to do was to reconcile with Melody, and I questioned if that would be the ethical path to take. In the end, I decided that I really wanted to be married to Melody and have our family. I ended my relationship with Eileen with deep and long-lasting regret.

I took away a painful realization that life has its limits, at times hard decisions must be made, and those about whom I care very much can be injured by my actions. I learned that I could not blame others for my behavior. No matter how innocent or naive, I am responsible for what I do and what I promise. I was forced to accept my failure and serious imperfections. It was a very expensive lesson, but one that I needed to learn.

With the crisis over in our marriage, Melody reactivated her search for meaningful career direction. She attended a psychodrama workshop and discovered that she truly enjoyed acting. Soon she gave up the idea of a therapeutic career and looked for a way to study theater and perform. She met people associated with the University of Chicago Court Theater and auditioned for parts in some of the plays that the theater produced. Soon she had some small parts and was working in production. This new direction made her very happy, and it shaped the rest of her life and mine.

As my time in Chicago ended, we began to look for where we would go and what we would do. I wanted to find a teaching position, but Melody wanted to study acting and have a chance to perform with a repertory company. This required compromise, because my best teaching possibilities were in small colleges, far from a major regional theater. Our choice of Chicago for my graduate work was mine, and I felt that I owed Melody the opportunity to pursue her interests. It was only fair after the sacrifice that she had made and the price we had paid for my Chicago choice, that her interests needed to be our top priority.

Our friend Fred Hudson once again entered into our lives. Fred had moved to San Francisco, where he held the position of dean of faculty at a small private school in the city. He suggested that I could perhaps get a teaching position with his school. At the same time, Melody could study in the American Conservatory Theater (ACT) apprentice program. Melody was excited about the possibility, and while we had no firm commitments from either Fred's school or ACT, we moved to San Francisco in August 1973. The year that followed challenged me once more and taught me a great deal more about the existing social attitudes toward blindness.

When we arrived in San Francisco, we had little money, no place to live, nor any source of income. Melody's mother, a recent widow, helped us financially, and we began to put our lives together in a new, strange city. Fred and Katy Hudson invited us to their home to swim in their pool, warm in their sauna, and draw encouragement from their friendship. However, Fred's suggestion that I might find employment at his college never materialized. Melody found that the ACT apprentice program had already admitted its class for the year, and Angie discovered that there were few children at her school who lived in our neighborhood, so getting settled in our new home was a difficult struggle. It was the year of the Patti Hearst kidnapping and the Zebra killings. The city seemed very unfriendly, and we had to fight to keep our spirits from collapsing into despair.

I began a job search in the Bay area, and Melody took first temporary work, and then a permanent position with an accounting firm. We found a wonderful apartment in the Pacific Heights area of the city, and Melody's mother helped us pay for it. Angie found a few friends, and we gradually started to build a life. Melody enrolled in a few classes taught by the actors in the ACT professional company and began to make friends. I found a friend from Chicago who lived and taught in the Stanford University community, down the peninsula in Palo Alto. I visited with him, and he connected me with the Stanford Career Placement Office, where I began to get leads on openings. I made contact with a Lions Club placement program in Oakland, where I first became a client, seeking placement services, and then later, a volunteer, running groups for job searchers. This experience would later pay large dividends. I read books on techniques for looking for a job and business management, and I continued to work on my dissertation. While I felt anxiety over finding employment, I stayed busy and productive and learned some new things that would later prove very useful.

Without a doubt, the most difficult, most frustrating thing that I have ever done is search for a job in San Francisco. I began by looking for public employment. The city of San Francisco had some job openings for which I seemed qualified. I went to the city building to fill out an application, but before I got to the personnel office, I had an accident that doomed my effort. The San Francisco municipal building has rows of columns in its large entryway. I hit my forehead on the corner of one of these pillars, cutting a deep gash in my head. Although I went on to the personnel office, I am sure that the appearance that I made was not a good one. I was not called back for an interview. Even though I was highly educated, had a good work record, was well dressed, and spoke well, I was blind, and I had a raw and bleeding cut on my forehead.

I made appointments with corporate personnel offices in the area, but never received more than a courteous, short interview. I applied for teaching positions at local institutions of higher education, and while in two cases I made the final cut, I was not hired. I met with a placement service that specialized in placing persons with disabilities. The service ran ads in the local newspapers and public service announcements on TV in which my credentials were featured. While I felt the announcements were condescending, I was willing to accept my inclusion in the ads if they produced some good results. However, they only led to one contact from an Amway dealer looking to build his pyramid of salespersons.

I contacted the California Division of Vocational Rehabilitation and enrolled for placement services. I was referred to a program in Oakland sponsored by the Lions Club. The Lions Clubs of America have a long-standing commitment to assist persons who are blind, and this program was a part of the charitable work of the organization. My first challenge was to learn to travel to the facility in Oakland. This required taking a bus to a downtown bus terminal, where I caught another bus that took me to Oakland. I would get off the bus and walk several blocks to the program. Perhaps one of the best parts of my otherwise frustrating job-search experience was learning to travel independently throughout the Bay area using various modes of public transportation.

My first meetings with the staff at the Lions center were promising. My counselor told me that he had connections with a major corporation in the area, where he felt he could place me. While employment with such a firm would drastically redefine my career goals, I was excited about the possibilities. Melody wanted to stay in San Francisco, and I could happily embrace a new challenge. I read some books that I thought would help me in an interview and on the job. However, I did not hear from my counselor for a week. When I called him to inquire about what was happening, he put me off. This went on for some time. Finally, I pressed him for some concrete information. He told me that the personnel manager at the firm said that none of the operational departments felt that a blind person could function successfully in their areas. This was an especially depressing piece of news. Melody and I had been excited about the possibilities of this job for our family. It could end our insecurity, give some permanence to our lives in San Francisco, and allow us to stop depending on her mother for support. It was devastating to hear that no matter how much I had worked or how successful I had been in the past, my blindness was a barrier that I could not overcome. I faced the possibility that I could not support my family or find productive work, and I could do nothing about it. I could not change the fact that I was blind, and it seemed that nothing else mattered.

I had no choice but to keep looking for work, and the Lions' Club program was a possible resource, so when the director asked me to volunteer at the center, I accepted his invitation. The center offered peer group meetings to discuss the job-search process, to explore personal goals, and to voice personal issues related to searching for employment. I had experience with facilitating small group discussions, and I had previously participated in one of the groups at the center, so I was given the task of organizing and conducting the peer group discussions. I had never worked with persons with disabilities before, with the exception of the one camping trip with the youth in Rochester. I had always avoided being drawn into a career that focused on serving persons with disabilities, because I wanted to be accepted as a normal person, and I felt such a career would be admitting that I could not compete in the mainstream world. However, my experience searching for a job led me to believe that, whether I liked it or not, my disability defined me as a person with similar social qualities as all other persons with disabilities. It was both a painful and a freeing recognition.

As I facilitated the groups and listened to the stories of the participants, I began to embrace the humanity of my colleagues. They were people who had lived real lives, had children, pursued dreams, suffered, and now they wanted a chance to become productive, financially independent persons. They had a dignity and integrity that I learned to respect. They were not lesser persons because they were blind. Their lives were not less important than those of persons without disabilities. I felt comfortable with them, and I felt a growing desire to advocate for the rights of persons with disabilities. I began to acquire an identity as a blind person who was a part of a community of other blind and disabled people. I had worked for many years for the rights of minority persons. Now I began to see that I needed to work for my own rights and the rights of others of my community.

In the past, I had believed that I was different from other persons with disabilities. The association with others embarrassed me. Somehow, I felt smarter and more competent than others with disabilities. I did not want to be labeled as a person with a disability, and thus by definition, inferior. I began to understand that no matter how hard I worked or how much I achieved, to the stranger, I was just a blind man. Like it or not, I was bonded to my brothers and sisters with disabilities. This was a huge turning point in my growth as a person and in my choice of a professional career.

In the early summer of 1974, I read two job announcements in the Stanford Career Placement Bulletin for openings at the University of California Riverside campus and the University of Colorado at Boulder. These positions were for the directors of services to students with disabilities. Although in the past I would have not been interested in such a position, by then my personal growth and development had prepared me to fill such a job. I applied for both jobs, but the University of Colorado's position developed more quickly, and in early August, I went to Boulder for an interview. A few days later, I was notified that I had been hired. Melody and I were disappointed to be leaving San Francisco, but the security attached to my employment was a decisive factor. I responded to the university with my acceptance of the offer, and we began to prepare to move to Boulder.

We said good-bye to the friends that we had made, sold our car, packed a few boxes for shipping, and gave our cat to a neighbor. We sent Angie to visit with her grandmother in Houston and boarded a plane for Denver. As we boarded the plane, I realized that a large chapter in my life was ending, and when we left the flight in Denver a new one would begin. I was both sad for the passing of my youth, and excited about moving into a new stage of adulthood. In the two hours that our flight took to cross from San Francisco to Denver, I transitioned from youthful student to responsible adult. For the past year, I had been neither student nor established adult. As an unemployed person, I had no established identity, but now I had responsible employment—a position with a university; a dream was coming true. I was ready for the challenge, but I wondered what would confront me on the other end of the flight.

On August 25, 1974, when we left San Francisco for Boulder, I was almost thirty-three years old. While I had grown up among other blind persons, the world that I confronted was very different than the one in which my family made their lives. I had learned to work on the farm where I grew up, and I recognized from my school days that a blind person needed to keep his hard knocks to himself. Along the way, I found that I was competent and strong. I tasted success and failure, joy and disappointment, happiness and despair. I worked to prove that as a blind person, I could compete with the sighted world, only to conclude that I really did not need to prove anything. It was all right to be a blind man. While I might have to hammer down some doors, I did not have to set myself off from my fellow blind and disabled peers. I wanted to engage the world, contribute to making society better, confront injustice where I could, and support those who were seeking to live lives of dignity and independence. I believed that I had prepared myself with the tools of education and experience that I needed to succeed, and I felt that I had a clear sense of my identity as a blind person and as an agent of social change. I had come a long way from the hill where I spent my early years, but I had brought a lot of it with me.

I knew that the new chapter would be challenging. I had been told during my interview that the position was a new one. Students had held a protest on the mall in front of the administration building the previous year to demand that an office be created to serve their needs. After some negotiation, the position was created, and I had been hired to provide those services. The largely inaccessible campus needed to be retrofitted so students with disabilities could use its facilities. Academic support programs needed to be created, and the acceptance of students with disabilities needed to be promoted among faculty, other students, and members of the larger community. As important as these services were, however, the most important role for the new director was to be a role model for the campus and community. I was expected to be an advocate and model for others, a spokesperson for the disabilities community, and a leader among persons with disabilities. It was a part of my personal goals and an expectation of those who had put themselves on the line to force the creation of the position that I take a leadership role in changing the perceptions of what it meant to be a disabled person. This was 1974. It was a time of greater activism among the disabilities community, and the new goals were independence, inclusion, and respect. It was my profound desire to be the kind of leader who could demonstrate a new definition of what it meant to be a person with a disability and assist others to also achieve that recognition.

When our plane landed, my transition was over. I was excited to start our new life. I was a husband, a father, and a leader in my community, and I cherished each of those roles. It was good to be a blind man, and I felt that my time had finally come.

CHAPTER 7

Settling In: 1974–1976

BOULDER IS A BEAUTIFUL COMMUNITY, set at the base of the Rocky Mountains where a mountain stream breaks out of the foothills and flows into the plains. Lying near the center of town, the University of Colorado features Italian provincial architecture and well-kept grounds. The Flatirons, a row of geological formations that live up to their name, provide a spectacular backdrop. When we came over the scenic outlook that provides a panoramic view of the city stretched out below, Melody caught her breath in astonishment. Our spirits were high, and we looked forward to making this unique place our own. Our student days were over. I had employment, and the future was exciting. This wonderful city would be our home, together and apart, for most of the next thirty years.

We took a room on campus at the University Club, and the next morning I began my employment while Melody searched for a place for us to live. My office was on the third floor of the student union. It consisted of two rooms, one that I used as a private office, and the other as an outer reception area. The Office of Services to Disabled Students, as the program was then known, was housed in these modest quarters for the next three years. This location reflected greater support from the students than it did from the administration.

Over the next several years, I worked to gain the approval of the campus administration. I believed that only with administration support could the program acquire the financial resources and institutional stability that it would need to survive and grow. In 1974, programs serving students with disabilities were few, and the participation of persons with disabilities on a college campus was still a new and untested idea. Many academics doubted that students with disabilities could do college-level work, and they resisted the suggestion that they might have to make accommodations. At this time, few were concerned about, or even aware of, title V of the 1973 Rehabilitation Act, which provided civil rights protections to students with disabilities in higher education. Section 504 of this Act would change the responsibilities of the University to its students with disabilities, but in 1974, this still lay in the future. In 1974, salesmanship and persuasion were more valuable tools than the weight of the federal law. It was not until the implementing regulations were signed into law in 1977, that Section 504 became effective.

Monday, August 26, 1974, was the first day of registration for the fall semester, and I spent the day at the field house, helping students make course selections, find accessible classrooms, and enroll. I knew little about the campus, so I had to make many phone calls to get the necessary information, but I met a number of the students with whom I would work over the next several years and began to learn the workings of the university. During the first week, I learned to move classes from inaccessible classrooms to ones that students who used wheelchairs could enter. I hired four students to assist in various ways and had my first interview with a reporter, who was following up on the story of the activism of the university's students with disabilities.

I began to build a file of Braille phone numbers, a procedure that I have continued until the present. I made Braille lists of things to do and started a log of expenditures so that I could ensure that I stayed within the office budget. This use of Braille was of the greatest assistance in operating as an independent college administrator. It is difficult to overstate how important the use of Braille is to a blind manager. No other single tool has been as important to me as I have progressed through my working life. I also began to set up meetings with the directors of offices that the students might use. I wanted to know about the services that these programs could offer, and I wanted my peers to understand that I was an independent person.

I always walked to their offices. Soon I became a recognizable person, walking across campus with my white cane. I wanted the campus community to know that a person with a disability could and should be an independent person. This message needs to be communicated over and over again. It is the responsibility of every person with a disability to maximize his or her independence, so when accommodations are requested, they are understood to be necessary. Those of us who have a disability have a right to participate in the mainstream of society, but we have a responsibility to contribute. We have a right to have the accommodations that we need, but we have the responsibility to take ownership for our own participation. While this philosophy demands responsibility from the person with a disability, it also promises freedom and self-respect. One will never be treated as an equal unless one acts responsibly. One should not hesitate to ask for assistance when it is genuinely needed, but one should equally not ask for assistance when he or she can handle the task independently. I made every attempt to teach this philosophy to the university community, and I think it found willing listeners among both the students with disabilities and the rest of the campus.

Within a week of our arrival, Melody found an apartment for us, Angie joined us and started school, and we found a big lovable white shepherd puppy. Melody explored possible acting opportunities, and we started to make new friends. Our next-door neighbors were Marion Robles and her two teenage children, Jo Ann and Glenn Ernst. Jo Ann would grow up to become a Stanford Business School graduate, world-renowned triathlon athlete, and wife of the bestselling author Jim Collins. We shared meals and played parlor games with the Robles-Ernst family, and Angie looked up to the older children. Soon we had a circle of friends, I got back to work on my dissertation, and we looked for more opportunities to connect with our new community.

In 1974, many of the students with disabilities were recent veterans from the Vietnam War. I spent many hours over the next several years talking with these young men and listening to their stories. A number of them were angry and frustrated, and some of them experienced genuine discrimination. One rather angry student received an injury that required one of his legs to be amputated above the knee. One day, as he was riding his bicycle in a dismount zone on campus, he was stopped and given a ticket. He was so infuriated by this treatment that he went to the campus police office, took off his prosthetic leg, and threw it down on the counter. He told the attendant that he had lost his leg fighting for America, and now he could not get the understanding needed to recognize that it was difficult for him to mount and dismount a bicycle. The police office called me and asked if I would take care of the situation. I went to the police station and brought the student back to my office. I talked with him for most of the rest of the afternoon. We, of course, got his ticket dismissed, but that afternoon I learned a great deal about the feelings of these former soldiers who went to war in good faith, only to return home to a very hostile reception. I vowed if ever I was in a position to welcome home another group of soldiers from another war, no matter how I felt about the war, I would do what I could to give them a better homecoming.

Another vet, a wheelchair user, applied for the medical technology program at the university's medical school. When he went for an interview, he was told that he could not reach the shelves where the materials were stored, so it was doubtful that he could be admitted. He told me that he had done everything that he could to become qualified, including having a 4.0 GPA, that he was married and had a new baby, and that he didn't know how he could support his family if he couldn't get the training offered at the medical school. He was angry, and so was I. I wrote a letter to the federal Office of Civil Rights and copied a long list of elected officials and university leaders. I stated the situation, allowed that no discrimination had yet occurred, and predicted that if this student were not admitted, there would probably be a complaint filed. The wrath of the university came down on me. A number of high-ranking officials told me that I was out of line, that such a letter was embarrassing to the university, and that there was no intention to discriminate against this student. The student was admitted and went on to have a successful career, ending up as the director of a lab for a major hospital in the Denver area. I never heard any more about the incident from the administration. When I wrote the letter, however, I was willing to be fired, although that alternative appears in retrospect to have been very unlikely.

Another student with whom I worked was quadriplegic as the result of a diving accident. He was enrolled in the college of architecture and was an artist and philosopher. He had successfully mastered many skills of daily living, could draw to a limited degree, and even volunteered to help a small group of local persons design a church for their congregation. He came into my office on numerous occasions to discuss life and the writings of the German philosopher Fredrik Nietzsche. He longed for an authentic being, but thought that his disability prevented him from achieving such an intensity of living. He said, "I feel so close to being that I could taste it, but I just can't get there."

I tried to tell him that it is the human condition that no one, able-bodied or not, can reach what Nietzsche had in mind. We discussed the meaning of human limitations. I told him that all people are limited. Those of us who have disabilities are more obviously limited in some ways, but those who are able-bodied are simply masking their limitations. Each person must make a life out of what is possible. The measure of a person is how well he or she takes advantage of his or her possibilities and accommodates to his or her limitations. This is as true for an able bodied person as it is for a person with a disability. He told me that he would think about what I said, but he never bought it. Months later, he learned to drive and purchased a van that was equipped for a wheelchair user. During the winter, he drove into the mountains, ran his van into a snowbank, got out of his vehicle, and was found the following day frozen to death. I never knew if his death was an accident or deliberate. Either way, I have not forgotten those conversations, which in a real way were struggles for the meaning of his life. He was an intense young man, struggling to make sense out of a senseless accident, and he just could not do it. I, on the other hand, deepened my understanding of the value of life in a way that helped me talk with many other persons with disabilities more effectively in the decades that followed. I am still grateful for his honesty and intellectual courage. He taught me to value life more deeply than I had before.

During my first year on campus, I met one of the university vice presidents. His name was Joe Johnson, and a few years later, he became the president of Grambling University, an historically black college in Louisiana. Joe and a number of his campus friends encouraged me to plan a conference for employers in the state to promote employment for persons with disabilities. They helped me to organize the conference and provided a little funding. This was an important event for me. Two things came out of it that genuinely changed my life. First, I met a number of leaders in the disabilities community from around Colorado, and second, the idea for an independent living center emerged from the conversations at the conference. Soon I was asked to join the steering committee for the statewide conference that would lead to the participation of Coloradoans in the White House conference on the Handicapped that would occur in June 1977. The second idea led in October 1977 to the creation of the Center for People with Disabilities, an organization with which I would be involved for twenty-seven years.

In 1975, Congress authorized the convening of a White House conference to study issues affecting handicapped persons. At that time, persons first language, for example, people with disabilities not disabled people, was not observed; nor had the disabilities community demanded that the term *handicapped* be replaced by *disability*. This shift in cultural sensibility would come in the 1980s. The congressional mandate instructed each state to elect delegates to the White House conference, and in Colorado, the decision was made by Governor Richard Lamm to allow a grassroots process determine who the delegates would be. In addition to selecting delegates, issue papers were to be developed that would identify important areas of need and concern for persons with disabilities. Federal JOBS money, through the federal Comprehensive

Employment and Training Act (CETA), was made available for the project, and a yearlong effort was set in motion.

I was appointed to chair the program committee, which involved drawing up the agenda for the two-day conference, arranging for speakers, determining the selection process for delegates to the White House conference, and chairing the debate on the recommendations that would be forwarded to the planning committee for the Washington conference. We conducted seven regional meetings across the state and took the better part of a year to put the state conference together. When we met in the fall of 1976, over seven hundred persons attended. Representatives from all regions of the state, as well as a cross section of persons with disabilities, participated. The conference thrust me into the mainstream of the disabilities community in the state and gave me the opportunity to meet state political and administrative leaders. I was selected to be a delegate to the White House conference, which the following year would bring me in contact with persons with disabilities from around the nation, as well as the national leadership in the disabilities community. The state and national conferences launched my involvement in advocacy for persons with disabilities.

During the winter of 1976, I heard a television news story about a blind woman whose name was Judy Miller. Ms. Miller had sued the Denver Board of Education for discrimination in its hiring practices. She was a recent graduate of the University of Colorado and held a credential to teach in the state. However, the school district would not hire her, because she was blind. A few days later, I received a call from the Denver School District. The caller wished to know if there were any students who might like to apply for a teaching position. The call seemed suspicious to me, so I called Ms. Miller and told her about it. This began a decades-long involvement with the National Federation of the Blind (NFB). Judy Miller was the Colorado president of the NFB, and she invited me to a meeting of the student chapter of the organization. I had met some NFB members in San Francisco and attended a meeting before leaving California to move to Colorado.

I had also been reading the *Braille Monitor*, the magazine of the national organization, so I had some familiarity with NFB policy and philosophy even before attending my first meeting in Colorado. The NFB became the organization in which I could express my interest in fighting discrimination, changing public policy, and writing about blindness. The NFB became a powerful force in my life, shaping many of my activities for the next twenty years.

In September, I attended the State Convention of the Colorado affiliate of the National Federation of the Blind and was elected to the post of first vice president. I spoke about the upcoming state conference on the handicapped and recruited a number of persons to attend. I was also chosen to attend a NAC demonstration. At the time, I did not know very much about NAC, the National Accreditation Council for Agencies Serving the Blind and Visually Impaired, but in the years ahead, I would become very familiar with it. The NFB offered me three very important experiences. First, it gave me a community of like-minded blind friends and colleagues with whom I could find support, develop friendships, and work to improve the lives of blind persons. Second, it provided an organizational structure in which I could learn and grow as a leader of the movement, and third, it provided a sophisticated leadership who were extremely effective in changing the social policies that limited the opportunities of blind persons. I grew to respect and cherish the organization and its members. It was, and is, the most positive influence in the lives of the blind in America.

While I was settling into my job at the university and developing my involvement in the community, Melody was pursuing opportunities to act. She auditioned at the Denver Center for the Performing Arts and the University of Colorado Shakespeare Festival, but she was not cast with either company. However, she did meet some people who were involved in the small theater community in Denver and got some small parts. She enjoyed her new friends, but was frustrated about her lack of work. She began to look for acting opportunities outside of Colorado, a search that would pay off for her in 1977. In the meantime, we made friends and embraced our new home in Boulder.

My office was next door to the office of the human rights program in the student union building. One of the persons who worked in that program was Mike Michener. Mike was an older student who was politically involved. He had worked in campaigns in California before coming back to school to finish his education. He was active with the Boulder County Democratic Party and invited me to a meeting of the organization's Affirmative Action Committee. As it turned out, this was the first meeting of the committee, and I was chosen to be its chairperson. This began a thirty-year involvement with the Boulder County Democratic Party. I met Dickie Lee Hullinghorst, who was the party chairperson at this meeting. Dickie Lee and her husband, Bob, would become my lifelong friends. We would support one another through decades of political activities. The most immediate effects of my endeavors with the county party were my attendance at county and state party events, including the state assembly, where I was a Frank Church for President delegate.

In 1976 the party submitted my name to the Boulder Board of County Commissioners for consideration for appointment to the Board of the Comprehensive Employment and Training Act (CETA) program. The commissioners appointed me, and I spent many years working with the CETA program and its successors. The CETA program provided funding for summer work experience for youth at risk, including youth with disabilities. Bob Hullinghorst and I applied for five positions with my office and with his program at the Western Interstate Commission on Higher Education. The positions were funded, and I received three of them. I used the positions to create a job bank for persons with disabilities, do an accessibility survey of the city of Boulder, and provide transportation services on campus. The student who created the job bank was Judy Mares, a young blind woman, who would become the cofounder and first executive director of the Center for People with Disabilities. A graduate student, Bob Radocy, in the recreational therapy program conducted the accessibility survey. Later Bob would become a successful entrepreneur, producing and marketing a prosthetic hand that he invented. A few years later, Judy and Bob were named to a list compiled by *Esquire* magazine of three hundred young Americans who were making a mark on society. Both Judy and Bob have had successful lives. I am proud of the small part that the Office of Services to Disabled Students played in their development.

During the winters of the first several years, we organized skiing classes for the students who were interested at a nearby ski resort. Blind skiers and students with other disabilities participated in the sport. I joined the students and learned a few things about skiing. We also sponsored some camping and kayaking activities. I wanted the students to be challenged to try new activities that would stretch them and help change the stereotypes about the abilities of persons with disabilities. I would promote adventure and challenge activities throughout the next two decades, both at the university and in my community involvement. We added rock climbing, sailing and rafting, horseback riding, and rope courses to the adventure education curriculum. These activities were among the most enjoyable and developmentally significant experiences that our students had. These activities were always conducted by professional leaders, who were well trained in the techniques of the sport and especially in the safety measures that were needed to ensure the safe participation of persons with disabilities. I am happy to say that we never had an accident.

During one of the skiing outings, I discussed with Judy Mares the idea of expanding the job bank program to include a broader range of services. She had been appointed to the CETA advisory board, holding a slot reserved for CETA consumers. At the time, her program was housed in the offices of the Boulder County Board for Developmental Disabilities. She wanted to have an independent program in a separate location. We discussed creating an independent living center. I read about the band of Berkley radical advocates for persons with disabilities who, led by Ed Roberts and Judy Heumann, had established the Center for Independent Living (CIL) in Berkley. Closer to home, a group led by Wade Blank had created the Atlantis Community in Denver. We evolved the concept of a Boulder County center for independent living that would continue to offer employment services, but would also advocate for needed changes at the community level, including transportation services, wheelchair accessibility, accessible and affordable housing, independent living skill training, and peer counseling. The center would provide a comfortable environment, where persons with disabilities could find the affirmation and assistance that they needed to become independent, productive persons.

We drew up a proposal for the program and began to look for funding. I arranged for Judy to receive a work-study grant from the financial aid office at the university to continue her job bank project, and we waited for a next round of funding for the CETA program. During the 1970s, the US economy was sluggish. The term *stagflation* became popular to describe both high unemployment and inflation. CETA was one of the responses to the economic hardship of the time. The program provided funding for the creation of public sector jobs, as well as job training and youth work experience. It was widely criticized for being inflationary, generating corrupt uses of the funds, and failing to create permanent jobs or teach durable job skills. To a large degree, these criticisms are probably true, but in Boulder County and specifically with the way in which we used the funds to promote independent living for persons with disabilities, the funds were very successful investments in the economy and social fabric of the community.

Our initial CETA grant funded five positions and provided money for office space, telephones, and a few other necessities. Judy and I recruited a board of directors for the new project, incorporated a private nonprofit corporation, and acquired IRS 501(c)(3) status for the Center for People with Disabilities. I was chosen to be the president of the board, and Judy was appointed its executive director. When the CETA funds became available in the fall of 1977, we were ready to start operations.

The Boulder County Center for People with Disabilities (CPWD) has been in operation for over thirty years. During that time, it has served tens of thousands of consumers. I count CPWD to be one of my very most important contributions. I chaired its board of directors for the first eight years of the program's existence. I left the board in 1985 only to avoid a conflict of interest, since I was a Boulder City Council member, and in that capacity, I provided public funds to the center. I returned to the board and to the position of chairperson for several more years during the first part of the decade of the 2000s.

CPWD has been important to me for several reasons. First and most important, its staff has opened doors to independent living and self-direction for a large number of persons who otherwise would have lived in nursing homes, with their families, or in institutional settings. These persons have experienced personal freedom that would have been denied to them without the services of the organization. Nearly as important has been the role that CPWD has played in redefining the attitudes of the community toward the inclusion of persons with disabilities in mainstream life. The agency has led in advocating for full accessibility. It has exerted a major influence in ensuring that persons with disabilities are employed, have transportation, participate in social and recreational activities, and express their voices in the work of local government. Persons with disabilities can live independently because of skills of daily living that they learn in CPWD classes. Many work because CPWD has broken down barriers to their employment. They live in the community because CPWD has helped them to find housing and to acquire home assistance that they need before they can leave a nursing home, and they are free and fulfilled people because CPWD has given them the hope and confidence that they need to take the risk to live independently. No life is perfect; living independently can be difficult, frustrating at times for a severely disabled person, but the opportunity to control one's own life is at the heart of what it means to be fully human, and I cherish it above all else for myself and for all others.

As I have said before, I cannot be happy for very long if I am not involved in academic pursuits of some variety. During the first two years of my life in Boulder, I continued to work on my dissertation, read widely in disability-related issues, and received several invitations to guest lecture in classes on campus. I also read Colorado history, acquainting myself with the major developments in the region's evolution from Spanish colony to high-technology leader. The fur trade, the gold rush, and the mining and ranching past create a dramatic narrative for the state's history, and I was captivated by it all. The rapid growth of the post-World War II period was changing the state from a Wild-West movie set to an ultramodern economy, and I felt that I was in the middle of it all.

During the summer of 1976, I read James Michener's book *Centennial*, a fictional account of the history of Colorado. Later that fall, Bob Radocy, working in my office, organized a camping trip for some of the students with disabilities to a site on the Arkansas River. I accompanied the outing and found some time to sit alone on the banks of the river, listen to the water, and reflect on my new home. Colorado is a beautiful state, and I was becoming acquainted with it. I loved the smells of the pines and the sounds of the mountain streams. There would be much more to come of outdoor Colorado, but by that time, I had already skied in the high mountains, hiked in mountain meadows, and felt the warm sun on a winter day. Colorado had a landscape and a history that thrilled me, and I was becoming a part of it. I came to Colorado with the idea of staying a year or two and looking for a new location, where I could teach, but I changed my plans on that riverbank. I realized that I had a challenging job in a beautiful environment, a growing set of friends, and a chance to grow professionally and as a person. I had found a new home.

If Boulder, Colorado, was becoming home for me, it was proving to be less fulfilling for Melody. She found a few small opportunities to work, but they were far less than the consistent, high-level professional work that she desired. She began to look for opportunities to act out of state. Toward the end of 1976, she reconnected with friends from San Francisco who helped her contact the directors of the Oregon Shakespeare Festival in Ashland, Oregon. They invited her to join the company, and as the year ended, she was excited to be moving to Ashland for the season, which ran from March to late September. She hoped that this would be the beginning of her entry into serious repertory theater. Angie would stay with me to finish the school year, and I would come to visit as I could. I was happy for her, but I dreaded the upcoming year. It seemed very hard for us to find a home where we could both find our place and be happy in our careers.

CHAPTER 8

Politics, Community, and
Separation: 1977–1980

T
HE YEAR 1977 BEGAN WITH the swearing in of Jimmy Carter and the coming to office of his star-crossed administration. The next four years would bring inflation and economic stagnation, the USSR's invasion of Afghanistan, and the seizure of the American embassy in Tehran. There would be an energy crisis and a post-Vietnam malaise. Predictions forecast the end of American dominance in the world, and Ronald Reagan became acceptable to the American electorate. It was a difficult passage for the American nation, and it was a challenging time for me, as well. I had some successes and some disappointments, and even failures, but in spite of the difficulties, I grew personally and professionally. It was a transition period. At the beginning, I was just getting settled in my new home, not widely known although building a positive reputation, and needing to confront the stereotyping associated with my blindness. However, by the end of 1980, I was prepared to launch a successful political career. I had established myself as a leader in the community, and I had begun my work with the College of Education at the University of Colorado. The four years were hard but rewarding, and I learned a great deal from them.

In March, Melody moved to Ashland, Oregon, for the summer season at the Oregon Shakespeare Festival. Angie stayed with me to finish the sixth grade and then joined her mother at the end of the school

113

year. Although I did not look forward to Melody being gone for seven months, I accepted and supported her decision. I found being a single parent of a twelve-year-old daughter to be trying. My responsibilities at work and in the community were growing. Neither of us was very good at cooking or doing other domestic chores, and I struggled to find the time to do everything. Angie and I had always been close, and there were moments when our time together was wonderful. We went to a neighborhood restaurant, where we became friendly with the owner. Angie read a book to me that she loved, and she enjoyed telling me about her adventures with her friends. We even learned to make a passable tuna casserole together. Still, when she left to join Melody, I felt some relief. I had a great deal to do, and I needed time to work. Perhaps I gave myself to my work at the expense of my family. In later years, Angie would say that I did, and I cannot say that she was wrong.

When the Carter administration came to power, members of the disabilities community were excited. In 1973, Congress passed a major rewrite of the Vocational Rehabilitation Act (PL 93-112). A key title of the Act, Title V, enacted the first federal civil rights protection for persons with disabilities. However, first the Nixon and then the Ford administrations refused to develop the regulations needed to enforce the act. Section 504 of Title V was especially crucial, because it had far-reaching implications. It prohibited discrimination against persons with disabilities in all programs that received federal funds in any form. This affected almost all state and local governments and educational institutions and most private nonprofit organizations. The lead department on the issuance of 504 regulations was the Department of Health, Education, and Welfare (HEW). All other departments would model their regulations on the HEW regulations.

As winter turned into spring, the disabilities community became restless. Meetings with Joseph Califano, the new Secretary of HEW, proved to be profoundly frustrating. He refused to sign the draft regulations that the disabilities community had negotiated with the previous secretary. In a monumental moment in the disabilities rights movement, members of the disabilities community across the nation took direct action. In

Washington, DC, and San Francisco, activists seized HEW buildings and locked themselves in, pledging to stay until the regulations were signed into law. In other regions, including Region VII in Denver, persons with disabilities organized protests at HEW headquarters, stating their demand that the regulations be signed.

I took part in the organization of the Denver protest, recruited other persons to attend, and spoke at the press conference. Over the next several days, we watched as the drama worked itself out. Finally, Secretary Califano agreed to sign the regulations, ushering in a new era in the civil rights of persons with disabilities. I studied the new regulations until I could recite from memory most of their provisions. The Government's Council on the Handicapped sponsored a statewide effort to do training for those affected by 504 and its new regulations. I was asked to chair a committee to develop and conduct the training. For the next year, I led 504 training workshops across Colorado, involving several hundred persons in daylong seminars. I was also invited to go to Washington to take part in the drafting of the 504 regulations for the Community Services Administration (CSA). I co-led the development of the University of Colorado at Boulder's transition plan, a plan for making the campus accessible, and advised and consulted with many other local governments and organizations throughout the next several years as 504 changed the landscape and opportunities for persons with disabilities. My work with the implementation of section 504 in Colorado marked my public emergence as an advocate for persons with disabilities.

In early June 1977, several thousand persons with disabilities gathered in Washington, DC, for the White House Conference on the Handicapped. I joined the Colorado delegation in the proceedings. President Carter spoke at the opening event, stating his commitment to advancing the civil rights and general well-being of the disabilities community. He related the story of his blind relative who made her life as a teacher in rural Georgia. Most of us were moved by his sincerity. Because of the positive impression that he made on me, I supported his reelection in 1980, even though Teddy Kennedy was popular in Boulder County.

Following the Carter address, the conference got down to the impossible task of sorting through and prioritizing thousands of recommendations that were produced by the state conferences. Soon a small group of delegates, led by NFB President Kenneth Jernigan, formed an alternative conference, aimed at simplifying the issues and focusing on a few areas where workable recommendations could be made. I joined the alternative conference, but remained active in the Colorado delegation, providing a liaison between the two groups.

To the best of my knowledge, very little policy direction came out of the White House conference. There were too many issues, too many disability groups, often with conflicting agendas, and too many demands for too few resources to create anything more than a large report that gathered dust on a few shelves in Washington. However, the gathering itself signaled that a large, energetic national movement was demanding to be heard and its issues taken seriously. In the end, the most significant aspect of my participation in the White House Conference on the Handicapped was my introduction to the leadership of the National Federation of the Blind. I met Kenneth Jernigan and Richard Edlund, the national treasurer of the organization, and many others as I carried out the low-level organizational tasks that I was assigned. The rhetorical talent, flexibility, and organizational skills of President Jernigan especially impressed me. He was self-assured and courteous, a gifted negotiator, and generous with his colleagues from other organizations. I was an active member of the NFB in Colorado, and I wanted to learn more about the national movement. That would soon happen.

Four weeks later, I traveled to New Orleans to attend the national convention of the National Federation of the Blind. This was my first NFB convention, and it made a tremendous impression on me. Almost two thousand blind persons attended. They came from across the nation to renew old friendships, learn about the activities of the national organization, make policy for the upcoming year, and most importantly, be inspired to take on the discrimination and cultural negativity that is a daily part of a blind person's existence. I got to know the Colorado delegates much better, enjoyed the attractions of New Orleans, and learned from the convention seminars and speeches. Once again, I listened to the powerful rhetoric of Kenneth Jernigan as he addressed the convention banquet. It is difficult to overstate how inspiring his remarks could be for a first-time listener who was discovering his identity as a blind person.

However, my most inspiring experience at the convention came when I happened into a room where a new film entitled *We Know Who We Are* was showing. The film was approximately thirty minutes long, and it ran continuously. I watched it at least four times. It said so much of what I had always believed about blindness, and it demonstrated how those beliefs could be implemented in a training program. The film was made at the Iowa Commission for the Blind, a state agency serving the blind, located in Des Moines, Iowa. Kenneth Jernigan was the director of the program, and the film showed him working with students at the commission. Blind persons wishing to live independently and find productive employment came to the commission to learn skills of blindness that would assist them to travel independently, read and write Braille, master domestic skills, and most significantly, develop positive attitudes toward their blindness and toward themselves. The film followed several students as they progressed through the program, confronted critical situations, and emerged as men and women ready to take their places in the larger world. I knew that I wanted to contribute to the liberation of persons with disabilities from lives of dependence and self-doubt to ones of freedom and productive independence. I went home to Boulder committed to find a way to make a difference in the lives of persons with disabilities.

Shortly after we returned from New Orleans, Judy Mares and I received invitations to attend a leadership seminar in Des Moines at the NFB national headquarters. Over the Labor Day weekend, we joined twenty or so others at the NFB national offices to learn more about the organization, its history and philosophy, and to tour the Iowa Commission for the Blind. Judy and I were already working together to create a program serving persons with disabilities, but the time we spent at the Iowa Commission for the Blind contributed to the final shape of our program. Our experience at the Iowa Commission confirmed our beliefs that a program serving persons with disabilities needs a strong philosophical commitment to independence, a belief in the capacity of disabled persons to direct their own lives, and an emphasis on productive employment. A month later, we opened the Center for People with Disabilities and operated it on the principles that we had drawn from our time in Des Moines. Two years later, we added a residential training program, which completed the Iowa Commission model. Thirty years later, the program is still largely in place as we designed it after the Labor Day seminar.

During the summer, I made the decision to run for the state legislature. A Republican woman represented the state house district in which I lived, and it was a traditionally Republican seat. It would be a hard race to win, but I thought I would have the advantage of having near-unanimous Democratic support, since few would consider running in the district. I got a list of the precinct committee people, Brailled it, and called the committee persons to ask for their support. Soon I had a corps of volunteers, and I began to build a campaign team.

In the early fall, the Boulder County Democratic Party sponsored a fund-raising picnic. I invited NFB members from around the state to come to the picnic, and thirty-forty of them came. At the picnic, I announced that I would be running for the forty-seventh district seat in the Colorado General Assembly. My first campaign was underway.

The first and perhaps largest challenge that I faced related to my blindness. I had to convince the voters that I was more than a novelty candidate. Serving in the legislature was serious business. It was a rough-and-tumble environment. One needed to have knowledge about a wide variety of issues, ranging from school finance to air quality, from welfare policy to the operations of the prisons in the state. I was young and blind, and my work and community involvement was, for the most part, oriented toward persons with disabilities. The question on everyone's mind was, "Can he do the job?" A second question, nearly as important, was, "Will he represent anyone other than persons with disabilities?" These questions in one form or another came up repeatedly, not only in my first campaign, but also in every one that I ever ran.

Voters asked me, "How can you do the reading?" "How can you evaluate budget documents, maps, and drawings, and the beauty of the land?" and "How will you know if someone is telling you the truth?" They asked how I would travel, dress myself, and find my seat. Sometimes the questions were trivial, and sometimes they were honest and searching. In almost all cases, they went to the heart of the fear that sighted persons have of blindness. I understood that I was dealing with the age-old fear of helplessness and dependency that society associates with blindness, so I dealt openly and factually with every question, no matter how trivial or demeaning I felt it to be. I knew that in most ways, these questions were not so much about me as they were about every blind or disabled person, and how I handled them would reflect on all of us, not just me.

In August, Angie returned to Boulder to begin school. She attended the first semester of that year in Boulder but after the Winter holiday she went to Ashland to live with Melody. In late September, Melody returned home for two months, before returning to Ashland for the winter theater season. During the visit, I concluded that she loved her theater world and would always want to make it her first priority. While she was in Boulder, she experienced two episodes of alcohol and marijuana-induced breaks with normal consciousness, which I found extremely troubling. When she left to return to Oregon, I felt that our marriage was over. I was sad but almost relieved. This time I was more assured. I knew that I could live alone, and I had so many exciting things to do. It came as an enormous surprise when a few months later, I told her of my decision to end our marriage, and she objected so sincerely, left the Shakespeare Festival, and returned home to help me with the campaign. I discovered that I still wanted our family, and the next several years were the best of our time together.

Melody and I worked together on my campaign, going door-to-door in the neighborhoods to speak with voters, hosting fund-raising events, and attending candidates' forums. She answered questions about what it was like to be married to a blind person and worked daily on all the minutiae that are involved with a political campaign. We made new friends, enjoyed the intensity of the political season, and even our thirteen-year-old daughter helped. When the election finally came, I was not surprised, but we were disappointed that I lost. The district was just too Republican for a Democrat to win, but I had made a good showing, dealt with the issue of blindness in a positive way, and reestablished my family. It felt less a defeat than a step toward a future goal. I did not know what that goal might be, but I did know that the world of political life was deeply interesting to me.

During the campaign, I realized that I needed to widen my political base and increase my knowledge of state and local issues. I needed to learn more about the environmental movement, water policies, growth in the Front Range of Colorado, and many others. I began my education in Colorado issues by resigning from the Boulder County Comprehensive Economic Training Act (CETA) Advisory Committee and applying for the county's Parks and Open Space Advisory Board. I was appointed and began a long and rewarding relationship with the open-space program of both the city and the county. The open-space program in Boulder County protects the area from urban sprawl, preserves agricultural land, and offers a valuable tool in the management of growth. It provides citizens with trails and peaceful outdoor experiences, as well as a better overall quality of life. It became a very popular program, and I enjoyed having a role, as a volunteer committee member, City Council member, and County Commissioner, in creating an open-space program that incorporated over eighty thousand acres in the two programs.

I also began a reading program. I increased my knowledge of Colorado history, read in the literature on the environmental movement, delved into writings on the energy crisis, and studied the state budget. A citizen activist and advocate for open space and environmental issues in general spent time with me going over proposed land-development projects and teaching me the context for the decisions that I would be called on to make. Her name was Martha Weiser, and she was the conscience of the community. She taught me a great deal about the history and management of growth in a fragile environment. But more importantly, she taught me to appreciate the responsibility that a public person has to preserve the environment for the generations to come. One must learn to balance short-term economic gains against long-range demands for the preservation of the air, water, and beauty of the land. The highest moral duty of an elected official or even of an appointee to an advisory committee is to get this balance right. Working with Mrs. Weiser was, above all, an advanced seminar in the ethics of public life.

While I worked in the community and ran for the state legislature, I continued to write my doctoral dissertation, and at the end of the winter quarter of 1979, the University of Chicago awarded me my doctoral degree. I felt a deep sense of accomplishment. I had made a commitment to myself over a decade before in Rochester to become a serious student, and through difficult and demanding times I kept my commitment. Receiving my degree gave me a boost in confidence. It was affirming to realize that I had earned a PhD from a university with an international reputation for excellence. I felt the intellectual equal to anyone with whom I worked. While I probably will never completely lose my feeling of being a blind, uneducated farm boy, the completion of my degree confirmed to me that I could compete at the highest levels of academic life.

During this period, I began to work with faculty members in the College of Education at the University of Colorado at Boulder. Terry and Nancy West teamed in a project to integrate the Education of Handicapped Children Act requirements into the teaching of the social foundations of education. They invited me to lecture to their classes. I prepared a paper, which I submitted for inclusion in a conference sponsored by the University of Minnesota, on disability and social foundations. My paper was chosen for inclusion in the conference and was later published with other conference papers in a book. This was, also, an affirming event. At the same time, I prepared a paper for the Rehabilitation Services Administration (RSA), which described the Center for People with Disabilities' new residential skills training program. RSA published the paper in its national magazine.

These opportunities to lecture and write were soon followed by an invitation to teach in the College of Education. Faculty members from the Social Foundations Program, led by Professor Richard Kraft, asked me to join their team. I received an adjunct appointment in the Graduate School of the University of Colorado and began an eighteen-year teaching relationship with the school. My work with Dick Kraft took me into the field of experiential education. Over the next two decades, in addition to teaching, I published a number of papers and taught in a three-year experimental teacher-certification program, which we called PROBE, for problem-based education. This program trained persons wishing to teach after having a first career. Some of my students from the 1980s are still active in the teaching profession. My academic experience with Dick Kraft and the College of Education has been among the happiest of my life.

In 1977, I began to work with Laura Fisher. Laura was a learning-disabilities specialist and an advocate for students with learning disabilities. At that time, there were few LD programs in the nation at the college level. Now they are pervasive. Students with learning disabilities have problems processing one or another sensory modality. They may have a deficit in spatial or auditory learning, or they may confuse written symbols. Many such persons test at a normal or higher level on most learning scales, but in one area or another, they have a significant deficit. Otherwise-intelligent persons are prevented from normal educational success due to their disabling limitation. Laura advocated for a program in the Office of Services to Students with Disabilities that would support students with learning disabilities. She argued that these students could learn methods of data processing that would allow them to compensate for their deficits. I worked with Laura to find funding to support an LD program, and while it seemed as if we would never convince the university that such a program was consistent with quality higher education, in time we built a major program that gained national recognition. Today's program at the University of Colorado at Boulder serves several hundred students with learning disabilities each year. By now, many thousands have graduated and gone on to successful careers.

As the decade of the seventies ended, my involvement with the National Federation of the Blind continued to grow. Diane McGeorge, the NFB of Colorado president, and I forged a strong alliance. We developed an aggressive advocacy program, successfully urging the State General Assembly to enact legislation that protected the civil rights of blind and disabled persons in housing, employment, public accommodations, voting, and insurance. We defended blind persons who experienced discrimination, worked to improve rehabilitation and educational services for blind children and adults, and worked to build a strong consumer organization throughout the state. Diane, I, and our families became close friends. She helped organize volunteers to work in my campaigns, and I helped her to break out of her career as a medical transcriber into one that challenged her potential to be a professional worker.

I also began to take on special projects for the national office. During these years, the national movement was engaged in a struggle with the affiliate in the state of Washington. The national board of directors chose to expel the leadership of the Washington affiliate and reorganize the state organization. I was asked to join a team sent in from out of state to work with Washingtonians loyal to the national movement to reorganize the affiliate, hold new elections, and nurture the new group. I traveled throughout the state with Dick Edlund, recruiting potential members, including Native Americans living on tribal lands, managed security at the organizing convention, and made follow-up visits to support the newly emerging group. I became the person in the NFB who managed the movement of large numbers of persons for demonstrations and conventions and other large gatherings. Often our marches involved one thousand or more blind persons. I also worked with local police and hotel security personnel to ensure the safety of participants. My role in these activities would grow during the 1980s as our numbers grew and our activities became more confrontational. This was an exciting and challenging time.

In the fall of 1979, I became involved in the campaign of B. J. Miller for Boulder City Council. She was a neighborhood activist and environmental advocate. She also had a strong social conscience and supported social programs and civil rights for lower-income persons. B. J. lost this election, although a decade later, she would win election to the City Council, where she would serve several terms. During the campaign, I met Tom and Enid Schantz, two political veterans who managed local campaigns and wrote outstanding political advertising. They became a leading force in my campaigns in the 1980s. Later, when I served on the City Council, B. J. Miller read my materials for council meetings on to tape. Her untiring commitment to providing me access to the council meeting packets allowed me to prepare for the meetings and participate on completely equal terms with all my sighted peers on the council. The amount of hours that she spent reading for me over a seven-year period cannot even be estimated. I am extremely grateful to her for her contribution to whatever success I had as a council member. I made friendships and found the political expertise that I needed to take my political efforts to a higher level in that 1979 campaign. The support of the Schantzes, B. J., and others whom I met in the campaign allowed my future campaigns to take on a polished, professional tone.

As 1980 began, I wanted to reenter the political arena. I continued to work at the state legislature on disability-related issues and dreamed of joining the General Assembly as an elected member. Melody and I had moved the year before, and our new home was in a different legislative district than the one in which I had run in 1978. The only problem was that a well-entrenched Democratic legislator represented the district. Chuck Howe was an attorney, a bit of a maverick, and very popular in the district. I joined the Boulder County steering committee for Jimmy Carter and waited for an opportunity. I did not have to wait long. Early in the new year, Rep. Howe announced that he would not seek reelection, and the seat became open.

I quickly assembled a campaign team and announced my candidacy. Soon after filing, I found that someone else had also been waiting for an opportunity to run in the fifty-third district. Ruth Wright was an environmental activist and attorney, and was very well connected in state and local Democratic politics. The reality of my position became clear to me as I learned more about Ruth. I did not know her, nor had

I even met her. I was a relative newcomer, and I did not travel in the same circles. I was a blind person, who worked within the disabilities community. I lacked access to the campaign funds or the political elites, and that level of party leadership believed that she had earned the seat because of her contributions. Had I known about Mrs. Wright's standing in the district, I would not have gotten into the race, but I did not really learn who she was until I was far into the campaign. In the years that followed, I discovered that Ruth Wright was an outstanding person, a gifted legislator, and a good and supportive friend, but at the time, she was a competitor and a barrier to the fulfillment of a dream.

Colorado uses a mixed caucus and primary election process to select its party candidates. The initial phase of the campaign involves selecting delegates at the precinct level, who will then attend a legislative district meeting, where they vote on candidates. If a candidate receives 20 percent of the delegate vote at the district assembly, he or she is placed on the primary ballot. In 1980, the district assembly occurred in early May and the primary in September. My campaign team got voter lists and began to identify friends and potential supporters in each precinct in the district. I made phone calls to voters, and we held house meetings in each precinct to meet with voters and identify supporters who would attend their precinct caucus and run to be a delegate at the district meeting. This was grassroots politics. While I started with a significant disadvantage, my team worked hard, and we lost the district vote by only four votes. We began the summer campaign almost even in the delegate vote, but those supporting me were less affluent and therefore less likely to vote in the primary, so I still was a substantial underdog.

A house district race involves a relatively small group of voters—in this race only about 4,500 persons voted in the September primary—so every voter is important. We had little money to do mass media advertising, so we printed up flyers targeted to specific groups—mobile homeowners and renters, apartment dwellers, university students, and other small groups of voters. We went door-to-door delivering the literature, and I walked the district, meeting voters. Tom and Enid Schantz wrote the flyers, giving them a literary polish that showed through their inexpensive production. Melody worked with me, and even fifteen-year-old Angie delivered flyers. The campaign was intense, but I enjoyed the closeness of my family and the campaign workers.

As the election grew near, it became obvious to campaign workers supporting Ruth Wright that the election was going to be very close and that their candidate might just lose. They organized an effort using well-known local Democrats to go door-to-door and raise the issue of my blindness. The charge was made that I would only represent blind persons. We knew that we needed to respond to this strategy if I was to have a chance to win. Tom and Enid prepared a large campaign ad, and we scraped up the money to pay for it. It focused in on just my eyes. A large headline read, "I'm blind. Let's talk about it." The text explained how I as a blind person appreciated the mountains and sky that give Boulder its unique beauty, outlined my commitment to education and other issues of importance to the district, and made the case that I was fully qualified to serve in the legislature. In the end, I lost the election by approximately one hundred votes, but what became known as the "I'm Blind" ad and the overall quality of my campaign changed my political stature in the community. At the end of the campaign, I was well-known, and I had gained the respect of the political leaders. Even though I had lost, I advanced my political career, and I think that I changed the community's attitudes concerning the capacity of persons who are blind and disabled to participate in life on equal footing with their able-bodied peers.

Near the end of the campaign, I began to understand at a personal level what some of the temptations are in political life. Two men came to my office with a proposition. The city of Boulder planned to use imminent-domain powers to take land for the construction of a shopping mall. My visitors opposed the city's plan. They owned some of the land under consideration and offered to fund my campaign for the legislature if I would support their effort to block the city initiative. I definitely could have used the money, but it would have been a political mistake of the first order had I accepted their offer. Apart from the ethical implications of the offer, I would have aligned myself with an unpopular cause and tarnished my reputation for acting in behalf of the public interest. It was a reputation of which I was very proud, and one that I wanted to retain.

The decision to decline the offer was not hard, but it alerted me to the trap that a political figure can fall into if he or she is lazy, greedy, or perhaps just careless. Once one starts to make choices that come close to the line, it is easy to take the next step. Campaigns are expensive, and it is hard to win without money. At the least, large amounts of money seldom come without the expectation of future favors, and the system of financing political campaigns permits a great deal of shady dealing. One has to feel the temptation of easy campaign money to really understand the danger to our democracy of the potential for corruption in the political process. A person cannot be a successful politician if he or she cannot raise large sums of campaign money. To do that and remain free from the influence of those who provide the money is a massive challenge for anyone who seeks public office. It is easy for the outsider to harshly judge the political figure who takes money for political favors—and these individuals must be judged—but if one has not faced the daunting task of funding even a small campaign and asking for contributions, one cannot understand the temptation to take whatever offer is made. I never got close to the line, but I never possessed the fund-raising skill to run successfully for higher office, either. Ethical commitments always come with a price, and one of the most serious challenges to a person in politics is to remain ethically centered while being financially viable as a political candidate.

In November, Jimmy Carter lost to Ronald Reagan. An era in American political culture ended. The domination of the liberal Democratic Party, which began in 1932, had run its course. A period of soul-searching and analysis was beginning, but for me, those last months of the year were ones of reorganization and anticipation. I did not know what my next step should be, but I was certain that there would definitely be a next political venture.

In the previous four years, I completed my doctoral studies, built an effective office serving students with disabilities, launched one of the first independent living centers in the country, began teaching in the School of Education, published two papers in major publications, emerged as a leading advocate for persons with disabilities in the state, and established myself as a leader in the local Democratic Party. My marriage had survived a major crisis, and I stood on the edge of an even more productive and challenging period of my life. I had absorbed defeat, disappointment, and pain. I had faced the doubt and discrimination related to my blindness, and I had overcome each of the barriers that had been placed in my path. As the year ended, I felt secure in myself and affirmed by my family and friends. In spite of some very real difficulties, it was a very good time.

CHAPTER 9

The First Term: Finding My Political Voice, 1981–1985

I BEGAN 1981 WITH UNCERTAINTY. While I was busy enough, I had no political voice. My program with students with disabilities was growing, I was teaching in the School of Education, I chaired the board of directors of the Center for People with Disabilities, and I had expanding responsibilities with the NFB. Still, I had no political goal. There seemed to be no opportunity for another try for the state legislature, and I wanted deeply to serve in elected office. My personal malaise was heightened by the coming to office of Ronald Reagan, the emerging of a national economic recession, and the promise of the new administration to overturn environmentally sensitive policies and take a more warlike stance in foreign affairs. While my life had many positive qualities, I felt helpless to affect policies that were important to me. I felt a strong sense of frustration, which disturbed an otherwise happy and productive life.

However, my life took a decisive turn in the spring. Melody and I attended a party at the home of Tom and Enid Schantz. While at the party, I met and talked with Paul Danish, a two-term member of the Boulder City Council. Paul was leaving the council at the end of the year and had announced that he would not seek a third term. He was a brilliant but controversial figure in Boulder politics, who played a leading role in limiting growth in the Boulder community. Paul, Tom, and Enid encouraged me to run for a vacant seat on the council.

There are nine seats on the Boulder City Council. Every two years, five of the nine seats are up for election. Four of the five seats receive a four-year term, while the fifth is only for two years. All candidates run at large in the city. The highest four vote-getters win the four-year terms, and the fifth highest serves for two years. In the fall of 1981, three incumbents would not seek reelection. This gave a newcomer a fighting chance to win a seat. I was excited about the possibility of serving on the City Council and told them that I would give it my most serious consideration.

Over the Fourth of July holiday, while I was out of town attending the national convention of the NFB, the local press reported the rumor that I was considering a run for City Council. When I returned home, I did not confirm the rumor, but Melody and I agreed that I would run. It would be my third election in four years, and I felt energized. My campaign team was in place, and they knew me well—something that is always a help in a political campaign—and I was comfortable with the demands of running for public office. My blindness had been fully aired in the previous campaign, and of course, I was widely known throughout the community. I needed to prepare myself on city issues, which I did by meeting with a number of well-informed citizens and city officials. I announced my candidacy in early September and launched the campaign.

I went door-to-door in the neighborhoods, leaving literature and speaking with voters. Going door-to-door is challenging for a blind person. A sighted volunteer worker always accompanied me. He or she would tell me which way the door on the house opened, so I could address the person directly when he or she opened the door. It is easy to look at someone when he or she speaks, but if the resident does not speak when he or she opens the door, I simply had to guess where to look. Still, I found the voters to be receptive and largely friendly. I think that they appreciated my effort to contact them, and we often had good conversations. I learned from them and used their knowledge and insight in the myriad of candidates' forums that are a part of local campaigns.

As the campaign developed over the fall, I found something to be happening that I enjoyed enormously. I discovered my political voice. I was in touch with the voters, I had relevant information ready, and I knew the issues. I gave answers to voters' questions that were short and to the point, and I felt confident. Few things are more fulfilling in a political campaign than to find your voice. The candidate can state clearly what he or she believes, and state it unapologetically. It is a feeling of harmony that makes running for office a joy. I found that joy in the City Council election of 1981, and it was thrilling.

When the election finally came, I finished second in a field of eleven, only four hundred votes behind the popular incumbent mayor. I asked for the chance to serve, and now it was up to me to perform. I knew that I could not please everyone, but I could prepare myself for every meeting, be responsive to those who wished to talk with me, and try to help when a citizen came to me with a personal problem with city government. I could be an advocate for low-income persons, renters, persons with disabilities, and others who had previously had a small voice with the council. I knew, however, that if I were to be an effective member of the council, I would have to master a wide range of issues. I would need to fully understand the budget and financial matters, city basic services, planning and zoning ordinances, and federal, state, and other local governments' relationships with the city of Boulder. I needed to understand the complex water laws that controlled the city's access to the water that it needed to serve the needs of the city, and above all, I needed to value the input of the citizens.

B. J. Miller read the materials for all the meetings. I attended conferences and seminars to learn what other cities were doing, and I listened to the citizens and to the city staff and my fellow council members. There was a great deal to learn, and I had to learn on the job. I knew, however, that I was not just representing myself; I was demonstrating in public view that a blind person can manage a complex job. How I performed would shape the attitudes of the city toward persons with disabilities. If a sighted person were not prepared, he or she would be judged lazy, but if I were not ready, it would be viewed to be proof that a blind person, no matter how intelligent, simply could not keep up with the workload. I served in elective office for the next fourteen years. I am sure that there were times when many, or even most, of the citizens of the city and county disagreed with my positions, but I never heard anyone say that I was not prepared or couldn't keep up with the workload.

I took the oath of office on January 1, 1982, and soon I was into the work of the council. Within three weeks of taking office, two events shook the Boulder community. A winter windstorm, with winds up to 130 miles per hour, brought damage to the city. Trees and power lines were blown down. Roofs were torn off houses, and a county government building was destroyed. Other council members were not available, so I spoke on behalf of the city to the press. While there was a good deal of damage caused by the storm, I believed that it was best not to overstate it. Work crews cleaned up the debris, insurance covered most of the damage to private property, and the county found other office space for its programs displaced by the storm. This experience early in my service in elected office proved to be important. Often the press looks for something sensational. One can be tempted into giving them what they want, but one can look foolish when the facts do not support an initial statement. This approach may not get you on TV, but it will give you credibility, and it is a much better approach by which public officials can formulate appropriate public policy.

The second event was tragic. Several firefighters were trapped in a burning building and killed. Their deaths were especially sad because the fire was a training exercise. I joined my fellow council members at the memorial service for these unfortunate public servants and grieved their loss. While public safety workers are seldom injured in the line of duty, their work always has the possibility to turn dangerous, and usually when it does, the results are catastrophic. A council member should never forget the risk that the community asks firefighters and police officers to take for the protection of the public. As I sat in that church and listened to the families sob, I became aware of just how important it was to respect and take seriously all those who serve the public. I always tried to give the city, and later, the county employees the support that they needed to do their jobs.

Ruth Corel was the mayor of Boulder during my first term. Ruth was in her late sixties, a strong and well-prepared leader and a social liberal. I admired her and her work. Boulder was, and still is, a well-to-do community, but it has a significant number of low-income persons. The city had an elitist reputation. Outsiders viewed the community to be both economically and culturally isolated from the rest of the state. I shared Ruth's concern that the city remain diverse and open to an economic and cultural mix of citizens. We supported affordable housing, social services, and renters' rights. Ruth was a role model for me. I learned from her how to support environmental policies such as growth management, open space, and height control without giving up a commitment to social justice. She was a powerful voice for civility in the public arena that is sadly lacking from today's public discourse. I learned a great deal from her leadership and from her clear understanding of the role of the mayor, the council, and the city staff. She argued that a mayor could only do what a majority of council members desire. Without four other votes, the mayor is helpless to act. When a mayor loses a majority on the council, it is time to retire, and in 1985, that was what she did.

As the year progressed, I dug into the work of serving on the City Council. It was a difficult time for the city budget, and we needed to control our expenditures. The city had a dedicated sales tax for the purchase and management of open-space land, and we had to set priorities for our purchases. There were the normal amount of requests for the approval of housing development and zoning changes. I was learning the day-to-day tasks of governing a city and enjoying the experience. However, in the summer, my political involvement took a major step forward. My friend and colleague in the School of Education, Richard Kraft, announced that he was a candidate for the second Congressional District seat on the state school board. This board makes educational policy for the state. Each Congressional District elects a representative, and one person runs at large. Dick asked me if I would manage his campaign. I accepted, and we began to organize for the fall.

He ran six years before and narrowly lost, but in the interim, the district boundaries were changed to take into account 1980 census data. Dick Kraft was a Democrat, and the new district was much more favorable for a Democratic candidate. Dick was unopposed in the primary and scored a landslide victory in the general election. In addition to gaining valuable campaign experience, I received an unexpected opportunity from his victory. His election placed him in a position to secure my appointment to the board of the Colorado School for the Deaf and Blind (CSDB). I became the first blind person ever to serve on the board in its 125-year history. I served on the board for a decade, acting as chairperson for over half of that period. Before my appointment, the Board of Education chairperson told Dick that it was board policy not to appoint a token blind person, and if there were a qualified blind individual, he or she could be appointed. Dick resisted the condescension and secured my appointment. My relationship with CSDB was long, challenging, ultimately successful, and personally rewarding.

Members of the National Federation of the Blind consider the organization's national convention, held each year around the week of the Fourth of July, to be the high point of their social year. Several thousand gather to visit with old friends, learn about current events in the blindness field, and be inspired by the eloquence of the speakers. The advocacy on behalf of blind persons is reported, and national political leaders who have supported the effort are honored. Convention week is exciting, enjoyable, and exhausting. In the years prior to 1982, the national leadership had given me an increasing role in the management of the convention. I looked forward to the week with great anticipation. Melody and I had attended the past four conventions together and enjoyed them very much, but a few weeks before the convention, she told me that she would not be attending. She had been instrumental in founding a theater for young actors, and the activities of her program would prevent her from attending. I was terribly disappointed, and as I dug deeper, I found that she never felt equal to others at the convention.

She felt that her sight, while useful to blind persons, kept her from playing a role as a first-class citizen in the organization. She said that she felt like a dog guide. I was deeply hurt by this revelation, and I believe this incident marked the end for our marriage.

In the next several years, Melody developed her theater company for young people, teaching, writing, and directing their productions. She also joined a theater group performing in Estes Park, Colorado, where she spent most of her time. I continued my work in Boulder, if anything becoming more involved at the university and in the community. She needed a life of her own, and I could not give up what I was building. My blindness was a complicating factor, because it gave me access to a community that she felt she could only join in part. Our divorce, finalized in 1987, came as no surprise. We never stopped caring about one another. We just stopped being a good match. Perhaps we never were, but our marriage lasted twenty-three years. We raised a healthy, mature daughter, and we supported one another as we searched for what we wanted to do with our lives. We certainly had our problems, but I learned a great deal from Melody. She gave me her support for over two decades, and she gave me a beautiful child. I hold her in high regard yet today.

In the fall of 1982, my daughter, Angie, and I went to Daytona Beach, Florida, where I led an NFB-sponsored demonstration aimed at protesting the efforts of the National Accreditation Council for Agencies serving the Blind and Visually Impaired (NAC). We opposed the efforts of NAC to take over the field of work with the blind. The primary issue was consumer participation. The NFB represented consumers of services, while NAC represented the established agencies. The agencies serving the blind were largely sheltered workshops and so-called lighthouses for the blind. The boards of directors of these agencies were made up of persons of privilege, who undoubtedly thought they were doing a good deed for the unfortunate blind. I met one of these persons on the street in Denver. I had just finished a meeting with the governor of the state, in which he and I discussed an important issue of significance to the city of Boulder. She said, "I am so sorry to see that you have to be out on the street by yourself. In New York we have housing and services, so the blind don't have to go out."

The condescension represented by the NAC board was insulting; the services that they accredited took away the independence of those they claimed to assist. The fight went on for years, and I organized protest demonstrations from Daytona to Little Rock, and Jackson, Mississippi, to Boston. We lobbied the Congress and the Department of Education, asking that federal funds and recognition not be given to NAC. Ultimately NAC became a nonfactor in the field of work with the blind.

Following the demonstration, Angie and I stopped in Missouri before returning to Colorado. The year before, my father was diagnosed with cancer. We spent several days with him. It was the last time that I saw him when he was able to communicate free of medications. On March 29, 1983, he died. My father had been my first and perhaps most important role model. He was a strong man with a curious mind, despite a lack of education. He had been a rodeo cowboy, a farmer, a police officer, and a corrections officer. He never stopped learning, and while I understood his limitations, I have always realized that I am fortunate that he was my father. I still miss him to this day.

While it had been almost twenty-five years since my father had been a daily presence in my life, I looked to him for approval. It had been a long time since I needed his help or since he could even help me, but his appreciation of my work remained important. When he died, I realized that I had to depend on myself for that final approval. At least in that regard, I was on my own. As we left the cemetery, I felt a flutter of anxiety in the pit of my stomach. He was gone, and I was fully in charge of my life. I was free from my father's judgment, but I was also on my own. I took a deep breath and went back to work. I felt ready to continue without him, but for that moment, at least, I experienced what philosophers call existential aloneness, and I was shaken.

I went back to Boulder, picked up my schedule of university work and council and community activities, and as I always do when I face a challenge, I read and thought. During the summer, I took some time off and spent it reading the philosopher and psychologist William James. Later I would turn my reading into an article on the ethics of William James, which was published in the *Journal of Experiential Education*, and then included in a collection of essays for use as a text for teaching courses in the field. I discovered in James an approach to life that I found instructive. He struggled with the meaning of life early in his career and found his meaning in a life of action. First in working, then in his wager that life was meaningful, he found the stability that he needed to create a productive career and fulfilling life. There were no prior certainties. One found value in life only by jumping into the stream and getting soaked in the life process. Maturity called for, in Paul Tillich's words, "the courage to be," and, James would add, "the courage to act." Underlying the Jamesian philosophy and psychology is the argument that all life and meaning is interconnected. In an essay in which he draws heavily on Walt Whitman's poem "Crossing Brooklyn Ferry," he explores the interconnectedness of the individual with nature, other life-forms, and past and future generations. The beauty of this essay and Whitman's poem restored my faith in our connectedness with all things, and I found the courage to be and act again. By the end of the summer, I was refreshed and committed to my path, wherever it might take me.

In the fall of 1983, the Democratic Party began to seriously look for a candidate to challenge Ronald Reagan in the following year. The leading hopeful was Walter Mondale. Many believed that if he were to have a chance of winning, the party would need to come together early behind a single candidate, avoiding a damaging primary battle. I agreed with this scenario and joined the Mondale team in Colorado. I was so alienated from Reagan policy that I wanted to do whatever I could to defeat him. Mondale was a liberal in the New Deal tradition, and I had admired him for a long time. It was an easy decision.

I was especially opposed to the Reagan administration's aggressive militarism in Central America, the escalation of the Cold War, deregulation of banking and big business, the attack on the protection of the environment, and the tax cuts that ran up the national deficit.

In Reagan cuts, the city of Boulder lost revenue-sharing funds that had been used to provide basic services. I considered the rise of the Christian right, one of the pillars of Reagan support, to be a danger to the basic principles of American democracy. My values called for a tolerant, open civil society, where political opponents could collaborate across party lines, but the growing anger and what appeared to me as inordinate self-righteousness were destroying the liberal American dream. The Mondale candidacy offered an alternative to the conservative vision of America that I readily embraced. In retrospect, this seems to have been a major turning point in American life and history. Liberal values and the liberal coalition that had controlled American public life since 1932 suffered an overwhelming defeat in 1984, but the dream was still alive in the fall of 1983.

The first blow to the Mondale candidacy came not from the Republicans but from within the Democratic Party. Gary Hart, a Colorado senator, announced his candidacy and quickly ran up a series of victories in early primaries and caucuses. Senator Hart directed the campaign of George McGovern in 1972, and as a Colorado senator, he had developed a reputation as a new age politician. I had met him on numerous occasions and found him to be rather aloof, but thoughtful and serious about his work, just as his public image painted him. He cultivated his image as a westerner, wearing cowboy boots and climbing on a horse whenever an occasion presented itself. He was the rugged outsider, but also a new man, looking to create policy in a postindustrial age and bring rationality to America's military establishment and foreign policy. He rejected the traditional base of the Democratic Party, which included organized labor, white urban ethnics, and the poor in favor of high tech sectors of the economy and upper middle-class progressive professionals. In part, this was because Mondale already tied up the traditional base, and of course, many of them had already migrated to Reagan, but it was also recognized that the old base was no longer able to command a majority in presidential politics. The country was changing, and the old liberal coalition did not have the same priorities as the new emerging groups. The new liberalism was concerned about the environment, women's rights, cultural freedom, and a more transparent democracy. The emphasis was on freedom, not equality, and opportunity, not social justice.

During the first week in March, I attended the National League of Cities legislative seminar in Washington, DC. Senator Hart swept the Maine caucuses while I attended the Washington event. As I flew back to Colorado, I felt a sense of disappointment and even despair. A month later, I spoke at the Democratic Party caucuses in Colorado on behalf of Walter Mondale, but Senator Hart won overwhelmingly in Colorado. I knew by then that even if Mondale won the nomination, he was not going to be successful in the fall. America had changed. The demographics and the economy were against him. A new generation and a new era in American life and politics was upon us. I did not like what was happening, but I knew that I had to adjust to the new reality. The Hart campaign finally crashed on Mondale's claim that it was empty of content, following Mondale's challenge, "Where's the beef?" and perhaps more importantly, when the primaries moved to the large industrial states, where Mondale's forces still had power.

The Mondale campaign demonstrated the vulnerability of the reliance of a candidacy on the largely working-class liberal coalition of the past, and that vulnerability was even more obvious in the fall election. The Hart candidacy was especially strong in Colorado, the senator's home state. All of the Democratic Party leadership supported him, so I found myself in an unpopular minority, but also in a leadership role, and before the campaign was over, I rose to the position of deputy director of the Colorado Mondale campaign. I organized an election rally in Boulder that was moderately attended, but a reporter summed up the campaign when he wrote that the Mondale supporters' hopes for a victory blew away with the autumn leaves in a park in central Boulder. On the Sunday before the election, the Boulder newspaper endorsed Walter Mondale. We sent the endorsement to the candidate, and we were told that it cheered him on an otherwise bleak day.

I worked hard for the Mondale campaign, but I was never optimistic about its success. One needed only to experience the frustration of trying to convince voters, and even friends, that the old liberal faith had any vitality left in it to realize that the nation had changed. It was a lesson that I would not forget. Still, I was glad that I had worked in the campaign. I got to see firsthand how a presidential campaign works. I argued nuclear policy, foreign affairs, and economic issues with Reagan supporters at churches, student gatherings, and political forums across the state. I was exhausted and disappointed at the end, but I knew that I had done my best, and that was comforting.

As 1984 ended, my old friend Judy Mares Dixon, the executive director of the Boulder County Center for People with Disabilities, told me that she was going to leave her position and take a new job with the Colorado Division of Vocational Rehabilitation. Judy and I had founded CPWD almost a decade before, and I knew that I would miss her. However, my tenure with CPWD also was soon to end. The Boulder City attorney believed that I had a conflict of interest both serving on the council and chairing the CPWD board of directors. The city provided funds for CPWD, and I voted on that allocation. While I regretted leaving, I knew that I must resign from the board. My last meeting was the February 1985 board meeting. I chaired the board for eight years and presided while the agency progressed from a concept to a program with a multimillion-dollar budget. CPWD was more than a service program. It was a source of hope for persons who wanted to live independently. I felt a genuine sense of loss leaving the center board. I knew that I would need to find another organization in which to invest my dream for independence for persons with disabilities. It would be three years before that opportunity would appear, but when it did, I was excited to grasp it. It came in the form of the Colorado Center for the Blind (CCB) and played an enormous role in my life. I shall discuss CCB more in the following chapter.

During the 1984–1985 academic year, I joined a team in the School of Education led by Richard Kraft that created an alternative teacher-certification program. This was PROBE. We used a problem-based methodology to educate our students. The students were given case studies that posed problems that teachers regularly face in the classroom, and they researched solutions to the problems. We met in small groups with the students to analyze the cases and the student research. Students did library research, but they also interviewed teachers, students, and other relevant players in the educational process. The students were persons who were making a career change, entering teaching after careers in other fields.

The PROBE experiment lasted for three years and proved to be successful. Our students found jobs and stayed in the profession, at least to the same degree as did students in the traditional teacher-training program. In addition to facilitating one of the small groups throughout each year, I supervised my students as they did their student teaching in the local school districts. While the PROBE program was successful and touched a group of professionals who normally would not become teachers, the PROBE team members had other commitments, so the program ended. While I worked with the PROBE program, I continued to direct the office for students with disabilities, served on the City Council, and worked with a number of community organizations. When we made the decision to end PROBE, I regretted closing a unique and creative experiment, but I also felt a sense of relief. This was an extremely demanding few years on my time and energy. I loved my work, but I am sure that I paid a price. I hardly ever just relaxed and let go of my obligations. I am somewhat better at relaxing now, but for better or worse, much of my life has been dominated by my work.

As 1985 progressed, my mind turned increasingly to my reelection campaign. Mayor Ruth Correll let it be known that she would not run for another term, and I saw that as an opportunity to take a more active leadership role in the community and grow as a person. It could also give me a more effective platform from which to make the case that a person with a disability could be a successful community leader. All council candidates run at large in the city of Boulder. The council members select the mayor. Traditionally the mayor was the top vote getter in the last election in which he or she ran, so it was very important to receive the most votes in the upcoming election. My goal in the November election was not to win a seat—a fifth-place finish would achieve that end; it was to finish first and position myself to be selected mayor.

After a snowstorm in late September forced me to cancel the kickoff of my campaign, the rest of the campaign ran smoothly. My team performed superbly, I earned endorsements from the major civic groups, and on Election Day, I was the top vote getter. I thought that I was in line to become mayor and looked forward to it with eager anticipation. However, my bubble was soon broken. As it turned out, my friend Linda Jorgensen had wanted to be mayor for some time. She was very close to Ruth Correll, and Mayor Correll supported her. Both Mayor Correll and another council member, Phil Stern, made comments to the press stating that they doubted that a blind person could adequately conduct a City Council meeting. Linda gathered a block of five, including herself, and I had four, including me. While the factors determining support for each of us were complex, there were issues of personal friendships and subtle ideological concerns that probably were crucial. However, those issues were difficult to talk about, so my blindness became the topic of discussion. No matter how hard I tried, I could not find a fifth vote, and Linda became mayor.

At the council organizing meeting, I nominated Linda, who was elected unanimously, and then I was elected deputy mayor. I was deeply disappointed, and I was hurt that my colleagues would use blindness as an issue. One of the realities that a person with a disability must accept is that no matter how successful and how well-qualified one is, his or her disability will always be a barrier. It is a fact that will not go away. It does no good to complain or feel sorry for oneself. It just has to be included in one's stock of knowledge. It requires a thick skin and an internal toughness to stay positive and let the pain go, but that is the only option if one wants to stay in the game. So I smiled, thanked everyone for their trust, and took over my role as deputy mayor. I enjoyed being Boulder's deputy mayor, and I genuinely enjoyed serving with my colleagues on the council. It must be said that there were members of the council who did not make blindness an issue, and in fact, supported me. Only those who publicly opposed me used blindness as an issue.

The years between 1981 and 1985 were tough ones. I had many losses. My marriage failed, my father died, the Mondale campaign was deeply disappointing, my long and personally rewarding connection with CPWD came to an end, and my effort to become mayor ended in painful frustration. Still, I was elected to the council and then to the position of deputy mayor, increased my teaching and writing, became more active in the NFB, and led the growth of the program serving students with disabilities at the university. I had found a voice to speak on behalf of issues for which I cared, and I had the confidence to make my voice heard. These were challenging, even highly demanding, years, but as I entered my second term on the council, I felt strong and determined. I was bruised and somewhat unhappy; yet I knew that I was resilient, and I was confident in my ability to continue to grow and face new challenges.

CHAPTER 10

The Second Term: Change and New Directions

S MY SECOND TERM ON the council began, I was unhappy and frustrated in my political career. I looked for change and hoped for opportunity to create a new path, but for the moment, I simply tackled the tasks at hand. The deputy mayor joined the mayor each week in a meeting with the city manager to set the agenda for the upcoming council meeting. At these meetings, policy direction for the city received its initial review. I continued to work with the National League of Cities, and my involvement with the Boulder Housing Authority grew. In addition to my work with the city, I carried a full-time load at the university, both teaching and directing the Office of Services to Students with Disabilities. I traveled extensively working on NFB projects, and I joined a community group that planned a sister-city project with Jalapa, Nicaragua. The year 1986 was a busy year, but it was only a transition to a career change and a more personally happy life.

During the 1980s, the Reagan administration escalated its involvement in the civil wars in Central America. The president supported right-wing forces in El Salvador and Nicaragua, casting the conflicts in global terms. He and his administration saw these conflicts as battlegrounds in the Cold War. Others viewed them to be genuine people's revolutions. It is difficult for a local government to have a role in foreign policy. The Constitution, after all, locates the authority to conduct foreign affairs in the executive branch, with some functions granted to the Congress. Still, many Boulder citizens, frustrated by the policies of the federal government in Central America, looked for a way to express their opposition, and they asked their City Council to help them.

I spoke at a rally on the university campus in opposition to the US involvement in El Salvador and Nicaragua, and let it be known that I would work with peace activists to develop a positive plan for assisting the people of Central America. Soon I was invited to a meeting of the group, and we began to plan a course of action. Over the next several years, we developed a relationship with a small town, Jalapa, in Nicaragua. Because of the political sensitivity of the effort, the City Council did not want a traditional sister-city arrangement, so we called it a friendship city. There were a few accusations that we were Communist sympathizers, but we managed to keep the project restricted to humanitarian work, and the larger community accepted the project, contributing generously to its efforts.

Over the course of the next several years, the group organized several truckloads of medical supplies and personal articles, which group members drove to Jalapa in northern Nicaragua. There were exchange visits between persons from Boulder and Jalapa. However, the largest project was the construction of a preschool, which was also used as a community center. I cochaired the committee to raise the funds to build the school. We put up a display outside the city hall, and whenever $500 was raised, we put in another brick until the target was reached. We raised over $30,000 for the school, and it was built. A number of Boulderites went to Jalapa to volunteer in the construction.

Many years later, while having my hair cut, I struck up a conversation with the woman who was my barber. As it turned out, she was from Jalapa, and as a child, she attended the preschool that I had helped to build. While the Jalapa Friendship City Project did not change US policy in Central America, it did allow people in our community who opposed the Reagan administration to find a way to make a positive statement and to actually help the people of a war-torn part of the world. The Jalapa project was truly an example of what is meant by the phrase, "Think globally, act locally." It was one of the most challenging and rewarding initiatives that I undertook while I served on the council.

In 1979, I formed a private nonprofit organization that was called Handicapped Media Inc. (HMI). The original purpose of HMI was to publish the *Handicapped Coloradoan*. The magazine was a quarterly publication that addressed issues of interest to the disabilities community in Colorado. We covered politics, the disabilities rights movement, and sports and recreation for persons with disabilities. During the winter of 1986, I attended the national Paralympics winter games in Jackson Hole, Wyoming, to write an article for the *Coloradoan*. There I met Paul DiBello, an athlete with a disability and trainer for the national team. Paul lost both his legs from frostbite in a mountaineering accident. In addition to training the national winter team and skiing, he wanted to develop a rock-climbing program for blind climbers. He challenged me to go climbing with him and then to build a climbing program for blind persons. I initially rejected the idea, but after further discussion, I agreed to try it. That began a decades'-long program that integrated rock climbing into a rehabilitation program for blind persons.

The Boulder area is a center for the sport of rock climbing. There are prime locations for climbing within a few miles of the city. In the summer, two blind students from the university and I joined Paul DiBello and two other trainers for a two-day climbing experiment. We learned to tie knots, put on our safety harness, provide protection for our fellow climbers, and make simple climbs. I realized that this experience could be enjoyable and challenging for blind persons. It could offer an adventure that could build confidence for persons who had never had an outdoor challenge. Two years later, we built it into the curriculum for the Colorado Center for the Blind.

I wrote about our rock-climbing experience for the *Handicapped Coloradoan*. The article was reprinted in both the blind press and mainstream media. Later, I received a letter from a man in India who wanted more information about the program. The local press covered our rock climbing, and a full-page picture of me on the side of a rock face appeared in the Boulder paper. Climbing was important for blind persons who were attempting to build the confidence to establish an independent life, but it also helped to defuse some of those public attitudes concerning the limited abilities of blind persons. Later we expanded the challenge program to include white-water rafting, cross-country skiing, horseback riding, and camping.

Melody and I spent the Christmas holidays with her mother in Houston, Texas. She was living and working in Estes Park, and we saw one another infrequently. We determined that it was time for us to end our marriage, and we told her mother while we were in Houston. We were sad, but in agreement that the time had come to make the break and find a more personally fulfilling life. Our daughter was grown and living on her own. We had our work, and we were beginning to establish other relationships. We could look back on over two decades of marriage in which we had been loved and nurtured by one another, but in which we had also been frustrated and unfulfilled. We chose to affirm the good and accept the bad, recognize our successes and forgive our failures. We filed for divorce as friends and remain so today.

On August 15, 1987, I remarried. I met Marci Carpenter at the National Federation of the Blind convention in 1982. She moved to Boulder, and I hired her to work in the Office of Services to Students with Disabilities. Marci had some residual vision, but she was legally blind. She shared my interests in politics and helped with the Kraft and Mondale campaigns. She involved herself with community activities and the NFB and became an important staff person in the disability services program at the university. Over the years, we were drawn together and fell in love. In time, I would find that Marci was susceptible to severe depression, and our marriage would end eight years later. However, for the first several years, we were very happy, and I felt a closeness that I had not felt for many years.

While having a wife who was blind brought with it some inconveniences (for example, she could not drive), it was a pleasure to share our involvement in the NFB, our experiences with the sighted world, and our attitudes toward sighted people. It was relaxing to live with someone who did not judge me for bumping into a chair or missing a spot when I was cleaning. I enjoyed living with another blind person, where I did not have to worry about living in the gaze of another. There is a subtle awareness of being watched that a blind person always recognizes and a tendency to depend on the sight of the other when a blind person lives with a sighted person that never completely disappears. The new freedom was exhilarating.

For many years, the NFB of Colorado and the Colorado Division of Vocational Rehabilitation (DVR) disputed the quality of rehabilitation services for blind persons in the state. During the summer of 1986, Diane McGeorge, the president of NFBC, and I made the decision to create a rehabilitation and training center that offered an alternative program to the one that the state conducted. However, we needed to have state support, because DVR controlled the funding for rehabilitation services. We went to the director of the state program and presented our proposal. While skeptical, he agreed to give us funding for a three-year trial program. One of the conditions of the grant was that we prepare a written plan for the center, including the philosophy and methodology that we would use. I agreed to write the plan.

The plan that I drafted was an expansion of the article that I had written the year before for the *Journal of Experiential Education* entitled "Transcendence and the Rehabilitation of the Blind." This book-length manuscript became the basis for the Colorado Center for the Blind. We used it as a training document, and a few years later, I was invited to Sweden to give a set of lectures to the National Federation of the Blind of Sweden based on my writing. I drew upon the work of the psychologist Eric Ericson to assert that the purpose of rehabilitation was to assist blind students to develop the ego strength needed to take control of their own lives, to shed dependency, and to become productive members of our society. I argued that all training needed to serve this end. Learning to travel independently, using a long white cane, mastering the use of Braille, developing home-management skills, and becoming computer-literate were but tools in developing the confidence and lifestyle needed to take control of one's own life. Rock climbing and other challenge activities stretched the student and contributed to the development of self-directed ego strength. The affirmation "I can make my own decisions and live my own life" is the beginning point for all independence, but one must also have the skills to make such an affirmation a reality. Our program wedded skill development with the building of ego strength. I spent much of the next decade nurturing this vision. The Colorado Center for the Blind (CCB) became one of the most successful rehabilitation programs for the blind in the nation, and is still so today.

We incorporated the CCB in 1987 and opened the program on January 1, 1988. Diane McGeorge became its first executive director, and I took the position of chairman of the board of directors. Over the years, blind persons of all ages came to the center to learn to be successful blind men and women. High school-age students came for summer training. College students, adults who lost their vision in midlife, and persons in their seventies and even one lady in her eighties entered the CCB program. The students lived in apartments where they were forced to cook and clean and care for themselves, travel to the center facility using public transportation, and work a full day in training. They discussed the meaning of blindness in their lives, how they viewed themselves as blind persons, and how the sighted world viewed them. They worked on skill development and set personal and career goals, and even took part-time jobs in order to get on-the-job training. The underlying driving force in all the CCB programs was a firm commitment to the belief that blind persons can live independent, productive lives if they possess the proper skills and have the confidence to take control of their own destinies. It was a belief that I had always had for myself, and it was the driving force underlying the National Federation of the Blind. I do not believe that any program serving the blind—or for that matter, anyone—can be successful if it does not embody this belief in its programs and personnel.

Marci and I worked together with the CCB and NFB, and it gave me great pleasure. We hosted students in our home, volunteered at the center, and went on the outdoor challenge outings. We attended national NFB conventions and organized NAC demonstrations. We met with state legislators to discuss issues affecting the blind community, and organized and attended seminars and retreats for blind schoolchildren. It was a productive and happy time for both of us, and at the end of 1987, another responsibility in the blindness community came to me. The State Board of Education appointed me to the board of directors of the Colorado School for the Deaf and Blind (CSDB).

CSDB was founded in 1873 and for over a century served deaf and blind children. When it was founded, the public perception was that deaf and blind persons had much in common, but nothing could be further from the truth. The two disabilities are very different. The two groups have an enormous amount of difficulty communicating, and because of this difficulty, they seldom interacted on the CSDB campus. Deaf and hard-of-hearing persons have a deaf culture that is grounded in the use of American Sign Language (ASL). Blind persons have no more access to that culture than do able-bodied individuals. The two schools exist on the same campus, but for the most part, they exist in parallel.

The deaf community and hearing parents of deaf children supported the school and considered it an important institution for their deaf culture. On the other hand, the school for the blind had become a school of last resort for blind children who had failed in an integrated setting. For the most part, blindness was not the only disabling condition that the blind children experienced. Many throughout the state were asking if a school for the deaf and blind was cost-effective or even consistent with educational philosophy, which emphasized inclusion in the least restrictive environment. When I joined the board, the school and the board were caught up in a bunker mentality, wondering if there were a future for the school.

Enrollment at CSDB shrank during the 1980s, causing teaching positions to be reduced, but instead of eliminating the positions, the school administration moved them to nonteaching staff status. The number of positions remained constant, even though the number of children attending CSDB fell. This did not please the state legislature. In addition, members of the adult blind community, led by the NFBC, were critical of the teaching policies related to blind children. The general feeling was that the school did not challenge the students or teach the adaptive skills that the children needed to become independent adults. The two most mentioned of these skill areas were independent travel using a long white cane and the use of Braille. The adult deaf community was also critical of CSDB practices. They feared that educational standards, and especially the use of ASL, were declining. Spurred on by the students at Gallaudet College, they lobbied for a deaf person to become superintendent of the school. With all of these problems, it was clear that the school was in trouble.

I spent time at the school, traveling to Colorado Springs each month for board meetings. I pushed to have the CSDB superintendent removed, a legislative cap set on enrollment, and a full review of staff positions conducted. I worked with the adult deaf community to present a united position to the legislature, and within a few years, I became the chairperson of the board. Over the next several years, new and dynamic leadership took over the management of the school, the state government stopped its discussion of school closing, new funding was found to remodel some of the older buildings, and a program review redesigned the educational offerings. I worked closely with the blind and deaf communities, the new superintendent, and the state department to create a team that could restructure the CSDB program and restore its credibility. I remained on the board for a decade, and I believe it was one of my most productive contributions.

In December 1987, I attended the annual convention of the National League of Cities (NLC). There I was introduced to the governor of Massachusetts and presidential candidate Michael Dukakis. I served on the Human Services Steering Committee of the NLC with Alice Wolfe, the mayor of Cambridge, Massachusetts. Alice was a Dukakis supporter, and she asked me to join the Dukakis effort. I readily agreed, and shortly after, joined the effort in Colorado. Drawing on my experience with the Mondale campaign, I was soon deeply involved in the presidential primary.

Campaign leaders asked me to take the position of chairperson for the second Congressional District. I was excited to be involved in a campaign that promised to compete forcefully and appeared to have a good chance to win the White House in the fall. During the late winter and early spring, Rev. Jessie Jackson made a strong bid for the Democratic Party nomination. In late March, he won the Wisconsin primary. The next stop in the campaign was in the Colorado caucuses the first week in April. For several weeks before the caucuses, Marci and I hosted two Dukakis national campaign workers. We ran the Congressional District campaign out of our home. On caucus night, we went to our caucus and were elected to the county convention, a path that would lead to the national convention in Atlanta. After the caucus, we went to the Dukakis headquarters to watch the results come in. We won the Congressional District and the state. We felt exhilarated, because Boulder and the second Congressional District was an area where Jessie Jackson should have had success. The Colorado victory seemed to turn the tide. It was quickly followed by major victories in New York, Ohio, and Indiana, and the battle was over.

Many of my closest friends were Jackson supporters. They asked me why I did not support someone who had been a leader in the civil rights movement and was a clear voice for liberal values. I thought a lot about that question and gave my answer in an opinion piece that appeared in the local newspaper the Sunday before the caucuses. I argued that presidential elections were about winning. It really did make a difference which party was elected, and the liberal vision of Jessie Jackson was no longer viable in American politics. The Mondale campaign made clear that a new vision was needed to turn back the conservative tide of Ronald Reagan, and I believed that Michael Dukakis had the best chance to reverse the conservative political culture that had taken control of American life. Dukakis appealed to a new America, which was more educated, driven by a postindustrial high tech economy, and in search of a smaller government presence in the nation's life. If these sensitivities were not acknowledged and respected, no Democratic candidate had a chance to win.

After the win in the Colorado caucuses, I briefly dreamed of looking for a position in a Dukakis administration. I imagined that it would be exciting to go to Washington and work at any level to address my issues, but this idle speculation soon ended in a most unexpected way. I received a call from Ron Steward, a friend and Boulder County Commissioner. He asked me if I would be interested in running for the Board of County Commissioners. A Republican held one of the seats on the three-person board. That seat was up for election, and no Democrat had come forward to run. I told him that I would think about it. Marci and I talked about it, and Ron organized a meeting with other Democratic elected officials in the county. We decided that I would make the run, and my political dreams became very real.

Boulder County is located about twenty miles northwest of Denver, on the edge of the Denver metropolitan area. It covers approximately 750 square miles that run from the plains to the Continental Divide. In 1988, it was home to 235,000 persons. In addition to the University of Colorado, it was becoming a high tech growth center. The county had been a productive agricultural area, but urban development was rapidly changing the character of the county. It had a strong environmental community, a strong element of the population who supported continued rapid growth, and a much smaller group of voters who clung to a more traditional conservative set of values. A strong but controversial group wanted to purchase agricultural land for conservation purposes, and a small but vocal portion of the community supported a social service and social justice agenda. Boulder County represented the newly emerging America, and I hoped that I could capture its essence, or at least enough of that essence, to fashion a victory in the fall. That was what I set out to do in April 1988.

In prior campaigns, I had all too often found myself in conflict with my friends, but this one was different. Most observers felt that my opponent was too strong to be beaten, so no one had come forward to take him on. When I entered the race, I found that I had universal support from the Democratic Party. Soon I had a campaign staff, and by the summer, the campaign was underway. My campaign manager, Gwenn Dooly, was an experienced campaigner, and Tom and Enid Schantz once again produced the media for me. Gwenn and I went throughout the county, meeting with groups, making speeches, and asking for financial support. As summer turned into fall, I began to sense that the voters were coming my way. I think most still thought that I would not win, but my confidence grew. Although my opponent was an incumbent, I felt that I had more information and could better handle the questions that the voters were asking at our candidate debates. My campaign events were drawing more people, and I was receiving enough financial support to run a credible media campaign. Still, on election night, there were doubts.

As the votes came in, it became clear that I was going to win. At the end, I received 52 percent to my opponent's 48 percent. I had what I had wanted for many years, a full-time political career. The County Commission directs county government. The county had over one thousand employees and a budget of over $50,000,000. The Board of Commissioners administered the government, set policy, and in some cases served in a quasi-judicial role. It was a job that was full of challenge and opportunity. I was truly excited with my victory and what it meant for my life.

Throughout the campaign, my blindness seldom came up. My opponent, confident that he would win, made little of it, but after he lost, he and his supporters spoke out. In an interview with the press, he stated that he did not think that a blind person could review the maps and drawings that are a necessary part of evaluating a planning or zoning policy issue or a request for approval of a development proposal. Letters to the editor reflected this claim. While I had been handling land-use issues as a member of the City Council for seven years, I now had a more central role as a county commissioner. There were three members of the commission, and not nine, as with the council. Often I would be the deciding vote when my colleagues did not agree about a proposal. I needed to demonstrate that I could make informed decisions. I knew that the land-use developers, the press, the county staff, and the public would closely watch me.

Land-use decisions are often controversial. Frequently there is a great deal of money at stake and treasured values may also be on the table, so one must competently deal with these matters if one desires to be reelected, and I certainly wanted a second term.

I met with staff in the Land-Use Department and talked with them about how I wanted to review documents. I have the capacity to conceptualize drawings and maps when I receive information about them. In some cases, I asked to have a staff person direct my fingers along the lines in a drawing, and in some cases, I went to the site and walked over it to get a feel for the land. I made note of measurements and did the math to get a sense of the size of a parcel of land, and I listened to people talk about what the project meant to them. Using these techniques, I believe that I never made an uninformed decision. I am sure that not all my decisions were correct, nor did I please everyone. However, I was always prepared, and I took into account the laws and regulations and the values of the community. After I took office, I never heard any comment that suggested that my blindness caused me to make an incorrect or incompetent decision.

In the two months between the election and taking office in January 1989, I took the time to go through the files in my university office. I had directed the program serving students with disabilities for over fourteen years, building the office from a one-person operation to one that employed seven professional staff persons and a number of part-time student workers. I was proud of the credibility that we had established both on campus and throughout the state and nation. I had come to the position with serious reservations, but I had learned to care for and identify with other persons with disabilities. I had matured as a manager, counselor, and program developer. I had used the office as a platform from which to become involved in the larger community, launch my political career, and begin my teaching role with the School of Education. My employment at the university had allowed me to support my family, meet many new friends, and do work that was deeply rewarding. It had exceeded my most optimistic expectations, and I left with some regret.

I also needed to wrap up my service on the Boulder City Council. I had learned an enormous amount about public affairs during the seven years that I had served on the council. For a number of years, I had chaired the city's audit committee, and I had participated in the making of seven budgets. This experience with public finance provided extremely valuable knowledge as I took on the duties of a county commissioner. I had been directly involved in land-use planning, economic-development efforts, and initiatives to provide more-affordable housing in a housing boom market. Boulder City government was creative and concerned with controlling the environmental damage brought on by rapid growth in a fragile environment. It attempted to address human service and economic injustice issues, and it strived to provide the basic services, fire protection, public safety, utilities, transportation facilities, and parks and recreation that citizens expect in a well-to-do, progressive city. The expectations were high, and in that cultural climate, the government was challenged. I felt that I had grown from the challenge, and I left the Boulder City Council feeling that I learned a great deal and served well. I had matured as a political leader, made many friends, and made important contributions to my community. The bruises from three years ago had healed. I was moving on to another position, but as I prepared to leave, I took time to acknowledge my debt to my colleagues and the citizens of the city. I was grateful for the valuable and wonderful experience.

The last two months of 1988 were covered with a happy glow. It felt like both an ending and a beginning. It was a genuine turning point in my life. Fourteen years earlier, I came to Boulder, and in the intervening years, I made a life. There was disappointment and pain, some failure and regret, but I met the challenges and overcame the barriers. I faced the personal and public doubts that my blindness evoked. However, the most important thing for me, personally, was that I never gave in to the problems that life continually presented. I faced my problems and worked through them. I continued to learn and grow as a person and a professional, and that gave me great satisfaction. I was happy in my personal life and excited about my new public role. It was a time of joy and celebration.

I looked forward to doing meaningful work both with the School of Education at the university and Boulder County, and my involvement with the CCB and CSDB promised to be challenging and rewarding. My daughter was grown and beginning to build a successful adult life, and Marci and I were happy in a new home. My mother came from Missouri for my swearing in. We wished that my father could have been there, but it meant a great deal to me to have her present at such a landmark day for me. She had worked hard to give me a chance in life, and having her present when I took the oath of office was a small way in which I could pay her back for all that she had done. I had traveled a long way since I had played on the hill in front of our house, but the lessons that I learned there had been valuable and true, and I wanted my mother to understand that I knew how that world had made me. No matter what others might think, my blind mother had helped me build a healthy and positive identity as a blind person, and I was proud of both of us.

CHAPTER 11

Years of Redirection: Politics, Rehabilitation, and Writing

I SERVED SIX YEARS AND eight months as a county commissioner. These were years of significant accomplishment, but they were also, at the end, years of deep sadness. When I left the position with Boulder County government, my life changed forever. I left to take the position of executive director of the Colorado Center for the Blind. The decision to leave county government had nothing to do with my experience as a county commissioner; rather, it was based in a personal crisis involving the dissolution of my marriage to Marci and the turmoil that I experienced as I tried to cope with her severe depression. Undoubtedly, I was not making good decisions, but at the time, I felt that I needed to escape from my surroundings and start again with something new. It was a time of extreme personal pain, and it took several years to fully recover. Once again, I felt alone. My dreams felt out of reach. Soon after leaving the county, I realized that I had made a mistake, but it was too late to go back. I needed to pick up the pieces and put my life back together, and over the next several years, that is what I did.

The Colorado statute that creates county government calls for the Board of Commissioners to consist of three members. When I began my service, I joined two other commissioners, who were widely respected and highly competent professionals. Josie Heath and Ron Stewart were friends and colleagues from past political battles. Josie was in her second term on the commission, and Ron was starting his second term. They were politically strong and personally admirable. I respected them and looked forward to serving with them. The next year, Josie resigned from the commission to make a run for the US Senate. However, Ron and I served together during the entire time that I was a member of the board. Our friendship deepened during this time, and we accomplished important changes in the county that continue to define the area twenty years later.

Boulder County lies at the northwest edge of the Denver metropolitan complex. Its natural beauty draws many who would like to make the area their home, but growth also threatens to destroy the very beauty that is so appealing. The arid climate adds to the fragility of the environment. Management of the growth in the area is a very high priority for any elected official, and Ron and I agreed that this was our common mission. We adopted land-use regulations that limited growth in the sensitive mountain region of the county, purchased thousands of acres of agricultural land for open space, worked with the cities in the county to manage their annexations for development, and planned a highway connecter to the new airport that would not encourage urban sprawl along its corridor. We facilitated the development of a countywide hazardous waste disposal site, instituted fees on new development that required growth to partially pay for its impact on roads and schools, and supported health and welfare programs that served low-income persons in Boulder County. We made improvements to county facilities, moved county government into the new era of the emerging computer technology, and controlled the growth of the county budget. I am genuinely proud of the many accomplishments that I had a part in during my time as a member of the Boulder County Board of Commissioners.

Commissioners are expected to travel around the county to oversee county activities and to meet with individuals and groups. The county provides a commissioner with a vehicle for his or her use in fulfilling these obligations. Since I could not drive, the county opened an account with the local cab company, and I was able to travel independently. The costs that I incurred while traveling were similar to those associated with the other commissioners, who were operating a county car. I used a Braille production service at the Boulder Library to prepare materials, and I used a reader who recorded documents onto tape. I spent many hours in the evenings and on the weekends to familiarize myself with the materials that I needed to do my work. I made sure that I was prepared for the meetings that I attended, and I was especially sure to be prepared for the official meetings of the board. Each year Ron and I rotated the duties of the chairperson of the Board of Commissioners. The chairperson conducts the official meetings. I used a Braille agenda to chair these meetings. Ron read some materials that I could not get in Braille. During public hearings, Ron called the names of those who had signed up to speak. The sensitivity of Ron and the county staff made my experience completely comfortable. The accommodations that I used were fully adequate, and my blindness never became an issue socially or professionally.

While my duties with Boulder County were demanding, I found time to continue my work with the NFB and the Colorado Center for the Blind (CCB). In the winter of 1990, a group from the Swedish National Federation of the Blind visited America to study rehabilitation programs. They came to the Colorado Center, and while they were there, I conducted a workshop for them, using the papers that I had written in preparation for the founding of the CCB. Shortly after their visit, I received an invitation to come to Sweden and deliver a set of lectures on the rehabilitation of the blind for the Swedish federation. I was excited to have this opportunity to share my ideas in an international setting, and in May of that year, Marci and I traveled to Stockholm. We spent a week in Sweden, lecturing and traveling. We met with leaders of the blindness community and learned about the services that were offered.

We were invited to make the case for a rehabilitation approach that emphasized the development of greater independence than did the more custodial Swedish system. The Swedish system stressed saving sight, and when this was not possible, blind persons were provided personal and financial support. Blind persons were not expected to work or live independently. Later, I would find this to be the philosophy governing services to the blind in Poland. Many of those who were comfortable with this approach were outspoken in their opposition to my philosophy, but younger persons, hoping for a more productive and fulfilling life, were excited about my message.

Since we were already in Europe, we decided to spend three more weeks exploring France and Germany. We spent a week in Paris and two weeks in Bavaria. This was my first visit to Europe, and I was thrilled to be there. We were two blind persons traveling alone in Europe, speaking little of the languages, and yet we used the trains and buses, toured the museums, shopped at the markets, and walked in the streets. We felt that we were living the philosophy of independence that we had espoused in Sweden. While this was a time of high adventure for me, it was the beginning of a difficult time for Marci.

Marci was reluctant to go to Sweden, and while we were there, she fell ill for several days. In Germany, she experienced a retina detachment, which required surgery to repair as soon as we returned home. I don't know if the demands of the month in Europe initiated her subsequent depression or if its onset had already begun, but the combination of illness and the stressful demands of the trip certainly marked a change in her health and in our relationship. We were living a big life. My political position placed us in the public eye, our travel and my writing and lecturing thrust us into an international setting, and she needed to withdraw from it. Although it took her almost three years to complete the separation from our expanding life, it began that spring, while I was experiencing such a personal triumph.

When we returned to Colorado from our European trip, Marci had surgery to repair her eye, and I went to the Colorado counties' annual meeting, where I was elected chairperson of the Front Range Counties Caucus of the state organization. Sadly, our lives were going in different directions. I chaired the Medicaid and Medicare Committee of the Health Policy Steering Committee of the National Association of

Counties (NACO). I often traveled with this position and testified on behalf of NACO before a Congressional committee. I continued to teach in the College of Education at the University of Colorado, chaired the boards for the Colorado School for the Deaf and Blind and the CCB, worked at the state and national levels with the National Federation of the Blind, and worked with a group that tried to mediate feelings over the war in Iraq.

When my reelection came in 1992, I was unopposed. It was a time of accomplishment and personal fulfillment. I was operating at a very high level. Others recognized my leadership ability, and I enjoyed the growing responsibility that was being given to me. It was the professional high point of my life. My blindness finally made little difference to anyone. My value to the community and the power that I held silenced the questions about blindness that had always pursued me. It was a happy time.

Unfortunately, my happiness did not last. When we returned from Europe, Marci began to withdraw from the many activities in which she was involved. I enjoyed our busy life and we had shared our involvements, but she no longer found our life to be what she wanted. Over the next three years, we moved apart, and in 1994, she filed for divorce.

Much has been written about the effects of mental illness on other family members. It can be devastating to a spouse, and in my case, it was. I thought we had built a life together that was exciting and challenging. We traveled and worked together on our many projects. We were prominent in our community, socially active, and professionally successful. I loved my wife, and I thought we were a happy couple. In the beginning, I recognized that Marci was experiencing depression, and I tried to be supportive. I encouraged her to get treatment, and I supported her decision to take some time off from school. However, this did not solve the problem. As we progressed into her illness, I found myself making excuses for her withdrawal. I hoped that things would get better and continued with my demanding schedule. As she

162

withdrew, we were less able to talk, and I lost track of just how serious her condition was becoming. She developed close friendships with some younger and less threatening persons. Our lives were unraveling, and I did not know how to stop what was happening.

I was frustrated, because I seemed powerless to communicate with her. I was angry, because she was throwing away our lives. I was hurt, because I felt betrayed. I felt alone, because I loved and missed her, and I felt frightened, because I felt that I needed to start my life over. Undoubtedly, I experienced a period of depression, although I did not seek treatment. My friends supported me and urged me to see a professional counselor, but I did not. I now believe that I would have been well served if I had taken their advice. When one person in a relationship suffers from mental illness, the other partner is left with all the responsibility for the relationship. Normal communication breaks down. The healthy partner cannot get answers to what went wrong. He or she is left alone to pick up the pieces of a broken life. It all seems so senseless and unnecessary. In such a complex set of emotions, the healthy partner is vulnerable. I certainly was, and it took several years to fully recover.

In April 1995, my friend and colleague Diane McGeorge announced that she was resigning from her position as executive director of the CCB. After some thought, I decided to take the position. I assumed my duties with CCB on September 1, 1995, ending a twenty-one-year residency in the Boulder community. I had been involved with the creation of the Colorado Center for the Blind from its very beginning. I believed deeply in its mission. I was quite familiar with its operation, and I felt very comfortable in taking up its management. Leaving Boulder for my new position seemed at the time to be a commitment to a more focused area of service. While limited in scope, I believed that I could make a greater difference in the lives of the persons that we served. Leaving Boulder gave me a chance to bury myself in a new home and a new job, to leave behind my painful memories, and to find a new life among the largely blind community, where I did not have to answer any questions about my blindness.

The CCB is a rehabilitation center serving blind men and women who wish to develop independence and self-sufficiency. They become students in the program, where they live in center-operated apartments and learn the alternative skills of blindness. Classes in independent travel, Braille, computer usage, homemaking skills, and confidence-building activities prepare students to live independently. Peer group discussions explore the students' attitudes toward blindness. Work experience introduces the student to possible opportunities for employment, and exposure to successful blind persons brings students into contact with positive role models. The program grew out of the positive philosophy toward blindness that characterizes the National Federation of the Blind. The CCB was a creation of the NFB and drew heavily on NFB support.

When I took over the leadership of the CCB, I was surprised to discover that it was in an organizational crisis. Revenue for the operation of the CCB came primarily from fees charged to state rehabilitation agencies for services to their clients who attended the training program. A breakdown in the relationships between CCB management and these state agencies had led to unwillingness on the part of state officials to send their clients to the CCB program, creating a financial crisis. The apartments where students lived failed to meet the standards of the Americans with Disabilities Act (ADA). Staffing for key programs was inadequate, and morale among staff was quite low. The program lacked many of the professional-level administrative tools and safeguards necessary to operate a responsible agency. I found that the first challenge that I faced was to establish the credibility of the agency among the state rehabilitation agencies that we served, the blind persons who were our students, and the CCB staff. While this was a daunting challenge, it was probably what I needed at the time, because it consumed my energy, making the transition much easier. I had little time to think about anything else other than solving the crisis at CCB.

In the next several months, I repaired the CCB. I worked with the staff to locate ADA-accessible apartments for the students, hired new staff, restructured our customer service training program, saving it from failure, traveled to a number of states to mend relationships with state vocational rehabilitation personnel, upgraded the salaries and benefits for the staff, and restored financial security to the agency. I threw myself into the program, and we began to achieve success with students whose disabilities had previously been too serious to successfully serve.

Many persons who are blind have other disabilities that are often more severe barriers to independence than is blindness. We discovered that most of the students who were referred to us also were contending with drug or alcohol addiction, traumatic brain injuries, or learning disabilities. This created conflict within the agency. The CCB was one of three similar agencies created by the National Federation of the Blind. In addition to the CCB, agencies in Louisiana and Minnesota have similar philosophies. The purpose of these agencies was to train a core of activists who could become leaders in the NFB movement. The NFB philosophy emphasized the centrality of blindness in one's life and the need to develop the alternative skills that will allow the blind individual to function competitively with his or her sighted peers. The NFB-sponsored centers were often referred to as boot camps for the blind. While the ideology was exciting, the reality was more complex. Persons who experience multiple disabilities must receive a holistic training experience if they are to benefit from rehabilitation. The needs of the individual must be placed ahead of the ideology of the organization. Many cherished beliefs must be examined. While Diane McGeorge was no longer the executive director of CCB, she was the president of the National Federation of the Blind of Colorado and actively involved in the collaboration between the two organizations. In time, this conflict would divide Mrs. McGeorge and me and cause me to withdraw from the CCB and the NFB.

In 1995, while I was a member of the County Commission, a delegation from Poland visited the three NFB training centers. When they were in Colorado, I conducted a seminar for them. Once again, I was invited to do training for the Polish National Association of the Blind, but this time in Europe. The three centers assembled teams of trainers, and I wrote a curriculum based on our common rehabilitation strategies. In the winter of 1996 and again in 1997, we conducted two two-week training seminars for the Polish Federation of the Blind. This was an enlightening experience. Poland was emerging from almost a half century of Soviet domination. The Marxist ideology had categorized blind persons as persons unable to live independently. In an effort to be humane, the Communist government had established sheltered workshops and special housing for the blind. Government subsidies and services ensured that blind persons lived modestly but comfortably. However, in the new era, funds were not available for the previous support system. For many, this new reality was the cause for anxiety and even bitterness. However, for others it created a spirit of liberation.

For the older generation, our message of independence was met with disbelief and hostility. They had never learned to travel independently, look for a job in the mainstream economy, or live in an inclusive community. They had lived lives of dependency, and they did not trust that any other life was possible. Our message of self-sufficiency and independence was greeted by the younger people with enthusiasm and hope for a brighter future. They wanted to receive mainstream schooling and create careers in the emerging Polish free enterprise economy. In the time that we had, we could not teach all the skills of blindness that they needed. What we could do was present a new vision of what is possible for blind persons in an open and free society. The credibility of our message depended on our ability to demonstrate our own skills and the degree to which our personal stories rang true. One can never know what the long-range effect of such training may be, but the enthusiastic responses from our Polish hosts left us all with a sense of accomplishment.

Shortly after returning home from Poland, my life took another unexpected turn. David Skaggs, the Congressman who represented the Colorado second Congressional District, announced that he would run for the US Senate. Boulder County was included in the district, and his seat was going to be open. Serving in Congress was a dream that I had always cherished, and therefore, I seized the opportunity. In the summer of 1997, I resigned my position with CCB, announced my candidacy for the 2nd Congressional District seat and moved back to Boulder.

During the following year, I worked to make my dream come true. Although in the end I was not successful, I needed to try. It is too easy for a blind person to play it safe, to not take a risk, to fail to pursue his or her dreams. I thought I would make a good member of Congress, and I thought I had a chance to win. It was frightening to put myself on the line, but I did not want to have to say that I did not have the courage or self-confidence to make the effort to achieve what had been a lifetime goal. It was a time in my life when I needed to define for myself just who I was. I am proud of my performance in that campaign. I learned a great deal about national politics, and I found that I did not have the financial resources to conduct a successful Congressional campaign nor do I have the ability to raise large amounts of money. The credibility of a Congressional campaign begins with its financial viability. While I raised over $125,000 in the Democratic primary, this was not nearly enough. I withdrew when I realized that I could not match the financial strength of my opponents.

Running for Congress is a full-time job. I opened an office and hired a staff. We set up meetings with potential supporters and financial contributors, attended meetings of all kinds where voters might be, spoke at candidates' forums, and spent countless hours on the telephone calling voters and donors. I went to Washington to meet with the national representatives of organizations that traditionally fund Democratic candidates, such as labor unions, civil rights groups, and women's organizations. I made speeches, sat for press interviews, and held fund-raising events. Colorado is a caucus state, so my staff and I contacted voters who might attend their neighborhood caucus. I placed second in the battle for caucus goers in a field of five candidates. It was a good showing, but not good enough in the light of my lack of funding. Therefore, after the caucuses in April 1998, I withdrew.

A blind candidate faces a number of challenges in a high-profile political campaign where there is high-level competition. One of the more difficult tasks for me is to work a noisy, crowded room. I found it important to have the assistance of an outgoing staff person. I would take the arm of my staff assistant, and we would mingle throughout the room. He or she would address an individual and introduce me. I would then pick up the conversation. In this way, I would meet and talk with all the attendees at the event. Not very many people feel comfortable meeting strangers and introducing themselves, but it is essential for a political candidate to possess the skills needed to present oneself in a competent and graceful way. Judgments are made on how one presents himself or herself in such a setting. It is difficult for a blind person to not look awkward. A blind and a sighted person must work well together to make it work. I believe it is something that my staff and I successfully mastered, but it took practice and discussion. My assistant needed to first be personally comfortable with mingling in a room full of strangers, and then he or she needed to be comfortable with a blind person. It is not easy.

In retrospect, I believe that I could have done better. I still believe that I could have been a successful Congressperson, but the stress associated with raising funds on a massive scale is something that I do not want to have as a constant part of my life. I reached for my dream and I failed, but I tried, and that gives me self-respect. Running for Congress was stressful and losing was painful, but not trying would have been to admit that I, as a blind person, needed to sit on the sidelines. Three other candidates in that race who lost were sighted. I did not let my blindness hold me back from trying. I lost, but it was not because I was blind. It was because the winner, now Senator Mark Udall, was a stronger candidate.

When I withdrew from the second Congressional District race in 1998, I was fifty-six years old. I no longer had a position with the University of Colorado, Boulder County, or the NFB or CCB. All of the intense involvements that structured my life for the past twenty-five years were gone. I needed a new career, and I needed a new purpose. I lived alone. My daughter was grown and had her own family. It was a time to rethink and redirect my life. It was not a time of crisis; rather, it was a time of transition and renewal. As I considered my options, I did what I always do in such in-between times: I read and wrote.

In 1979, a few friends and I founded a private, nonprofit organization that we called Handicapped Media Inc. (later incorporated as Disability Media Inc. in recognition of the changing terminology associated with persons with disabilities). During the past two decades, I worked with DMI to publish a magazine aimed at the disabilities community in Colorado. The project had been only a minor part of my activities to that point, but I had always enjoyed writing and publishing the magazine, and I concluded that expanding the operation might be something that I would find worthwhile. With that decision, I launched a new career and a new direction for my life. Over the last fifteen years, my primary purpose in my work has been to tell the story of the disabilities community, to bring forth to the whole society the full humanity of persons with disabilities, and to provide outlets for others to tell their unique stories of struggle and success as they insert themselves into the mainstream of life. It has been a challenge to learn the business, find the funding to operate a publishing operation, and produce the material that we need for publication, but the effort has been rewarding. It has given me purpose as I approach the final decades of my life, and it has brought me together with a partner who gives me great joy.

Angie Wood and I worked together at the Colorado Center for the Blind. She held the position of assistant director, while I held the lead position. When I left the CCB to run for Congress, Angie sought to become the director. However, in a bruising process, she was passed over, and Diane McGeorge regained the position. Angie is sighted, and that was deemed to disqualify her for leadership of an agency serving blind clients. Although Diane's past performance and health made her a poor candidate (she resigned within a few months), the CCB Board of Directors chose her to direct the agency. She viciously attacked Angie in order to secure the appointment. Angie left her employment with sadness and grief. Angie worked with me on my Congressional campaign and looked for career opportunities. When I left the race, we decided to form a business that would take us into the production of media aimed at the disabilities community. We called the new corporation A&H Publishing, and for the next five years, we published two magazines and experimented with a book.

We initiated a magazine that we called *Disability Life* and developed a national circulation. *Disability Life* was a glossy, full-color publication. In addition to a mailing list, we arranged for the Borders bookstore to carry our magazine. Angie edited *Disability Life* and provided many of the photographs. I did most of the writing. I wrote articles dealing with important social and political issues, the advocacy of activist disability groups, travel, and short fiction. We solicited material from leading members of the disabilities community and political figures. Congressman Mark Udall gave us an article, and so did Federal Court Judge John Cane. Our motto for the magazine was "Changing old myths into new realities," and that was our message. We told the story of a community that was taking control of its own destiny and claiming its rightful place in an inclusive social order.

We called our second magazine the *Colorado Quarterly*. Our editor was an old friend and colleague from my political career. Margi Ness was a community activist and world traveler. She brought an international perspective to our publication. While the *Colorado Quarterly* was aimed at a state audience, Margi shared with our readers her perceptions of the Latin American disabilities community. While I did a majority of the writing for the *Colorado Quarterly*, Margi and others made substantial contributions. Our magazine became a source of information and discussion throughout the state. Each issue focused on an independent living center, and we included an interview with a leader in the state. The publication of these two magazines brought me into contact with many of the state and national leaders in the disabilities community and gave me an opportunity to think about the meaning of disability in our society. It was a deeply rewarding time of personal growth.

Publishing was only one of the projects that I initiated during these years. I returned to the board of directors of the Center for People with Disabilities, was appointed to the Statewide Independent Living Council, joined the Board of Commissioners for the Boulder County Housing Authority, and worked as a consultant to the Colorado School for the Deaf and Blind. I also agreed to join the board of directors of CDR, a Boulder-based organization that focused on mediation training and dispute management. CDR marketed its services to an international client base. Its staff worked in Latin America, the Middle East, and Canada, as well as in the United States. It was very stimulating to interact with a group of highly skilled professionals in the field of mediation and dispute resolution. I was engaged in a new set of projects, which were stimulating and challenging, and as my sixtieth birthday came in October 2001, I could honestly say that I was living in one of the most creative and productive times of my life.

The Statewide Independent Living Council (SILC), a citizen council mandated in the federal Vocational Rehabilitation Act to promote independent living, issued a request for proposals for a coordinator of advocacy activities. I submitted a proposal, and HMI was chosen to receive the contract. I coordinated the activities of the Colorado SILC from 2002 to 2004, working closely with the State Vocational Rehabilitation agency, the members of SILC, the ten independent living centers in the state, and other groups of persons with disabilities. I conducted training for the ILC boards of directors and organized community seminars throughout the state that addressed community needs. I worked with the Colorado Medicaid program to increase opportunities for persons with disabilities in nursing homes to live in integrated settings, and I organized efforts to educate legislators concerning the importance of support for independent living. I wrote the Statewide Plan for Independent Living (SPIL) in 2004. The federal statute creating the independent living program requires that each state receiving federal independent living funds submit a SPIL every three years. The plan must be approved if the state is to receive funds. Our plan was approved, and the much-needed money flowed into the state.

As I moved into my new career, I discovered that I needed to learn new skills. Prior to 1998, I had not used the new computer technology, but now with all the writing and editing that I was doing, I needed to become computer-literate and master the accommodations that provide computer accessibility to blind users. I initially wrote my articles in Braille and then read them to an assistant, who entered the text into a computer. This process was time-consuming and inconvenient. I needed to take the time and make the effort to learn how to use computer technology. When I became proficient enough to use my computer, I found that it was a truly valuable tool. The new technology provides a blind person with a level of independence never before imagined. I have independent access to print materials on the Internet, and I can download books and articles in substantial quantities. I can correspond with friends and business associates without the assistance of a reader. I often wonder how things might have turned out if I could have read the letters from girlfriends so many years ago. E-mail opens up a new world of independent interaction with others. The freedom and independence that I have achieved from gaining access to computer technology have been of great value to me personally and professionally.

Perhaps the greatest challenge for our publishing enterprise was the development of a dependable funding source. Advertising could only produce a small portion of the needed revenue to cover the costs of printing and mailing, writing and editing, and supplies and travel, all essential costs. Fortunately, we were able to use a fund-raising opportunity that is available to charitable organizations in Colorado. We were able to conduct bingo sessions. This source of revenue allowed the publication of our magazines until we chose to stop publishing in 2004.

In Colorado, private nonprofit organizations can conduct bingo and use the proceeds to operate the charitable activities for which the organization has been chartered. In our case, this purpose was the production of educational materials for persons with disabilities. We were able to raise approximately $200,000 a year through the bingo program, and that made the magazine publishing effort possible. We teamed with another charitable organization to share the work involved in conducting bingo. The two organizations pooled our volunteer resources so that we could staff the rather labor-intensive bingo sessions, and in that way we were able to operate the effort for over five years.

A charitable organization must rent space in a bingo hall to conduct its sessions. The sessions last approximately three hours, so many sessions can be conducted during a week. We recognized that we were paying a good deal of our revenue to the hall where we were operating our bingo games, so we determined to invest in a hall, where we could conduct our sessions and also provide a venue for other nonprofit groups to raise funds for their programs. In June 2000, we took over the management of Winner's Bingo, a hall in Aurora, Colorado, and began the operation of a business that continues to the present. Winner's Bingo is a small business, and we have gone through all the problems that every small business faces. I have learned a great deal from the management of this enterprise. We have struggled with cash flow, retaining a high-quality workforce, marketing our hall to renters and customers, maintaining the property, and dealing with the neighbors. Yet the business has been a success and is profitable. We have assisted many nonprofit organizations to carry out their missions. Religious organizations, auxiliary high school activities, private schools, youth sports programs, and community improvement groups are just some of the types of organizations that we have helped to fund their activities. I took the lead role in the management of Winner's Bingo until 2004, but since that date, Angie has been the managing partner.

I spent most of my career in the public sector, but through my work with Winner's Bingo, I have gotten hands-on experience with the challenges of operating a private business. In truth, there is little difference. Revenue must cover expenses. The work of the organization must get done. Bills must be paid and payroll met, and consumers satisfied. The challenges of leading an organization, whether it is governmental, private nonprofit, or for-profit, are stressful, and when successfully met, rewarding. I have enjoyed the challenges of each setting.

Late in 2003, my life took yet another turn. Over the years, Angie and I grew closer together, and by the fall of 2003, we concluded that we were committed to one another. We made the decision to retire and move to another part of the country. We wanted a little land, where we could keep some animals, have a garden and some fruit trees, and live a slower-paced life. After a good deal of research, we chose the Columbia, Missouri, area to relocate.

Early in 2004, we went to Columbia to search for a new home. We found an eleven-acre parcel with a house and barn, a pond, and a small orchard. It fit our requirements perfectly, and we bought it.

Over the next several months, we wrapped up our business. I wrote the Statewide Plan for Independent Living (SPIL) and submitted it to the Rehabilitation Services Administration for approval. We terminated the publication of our magazines, and I resigned from the boards and commissions on which I served. We arranged to manage Winner's Bingo from Missouri, and I said farewell to my Colorado friends. I had lived in Colorado for thirty years. I had experienced many successes and many unhappy moments. I had come to the state to start my career, and now I was leaving to move into retirement. It was a time of reflection and regret for missed opportunities, but it was also a time of happiness.

As I prepared to leave my home of three decades, I realized that my life was very full. I had not sat on the sidelines. I had been a player. I had accepted the challenges of my work and of my personal life and met them responsibly and with as much competence as I possessed. In spite of failures and disappointments, I could affirm my actions and decisions. Now I was ready to start a new chapter of my life with someone whom I trusted and loved very deeply. I shipped my furniture to my new home in Missouri, and on May 1, 2004, we packed up our car and drove to Columbia.

CHAPTER 12

The Intersection of Aging and Disability

I WAS EXCITED ABOUT MOVING back to Columbia, Missouri. Columbia had been the site of so many experiences that contributed to my growing into adulthood. I had loved my years at the University of Missouri and the involvement that I had in the community. It was a coming home. While Angie did not share any memories of the Columbia area, she was willing to build our life together in the region. However, in spite of our plans, they were not to be easily realized. We were never to live on our dream property, and it would be five years before we could make our home together in Columbia.

Angie's mother suffered from congestive obstructive pulmonary disorder (COPD). She was in declining health, and we wanted her to move to Missouri so Angie could care for her. However, she refused to move and Angie felt intensely guilty about leaving her. She chose to return to Colorado to care for her mother. She lived with her and cared for her until her death five years later. It was not until 2009 that she could join me. We were married on November 7, 2009, but by that time, I had been forced to sell our country property and purchase a home in the city because alternative transportation was not available to me outside the city.

I understood the conflict that Angie faced. She was torn between starting a new life and caring for an ill and aging parent. I accepted and supported her decision to care for her mother, even though it cut into the years that we had to build our life together. When she moved to Columbia, she was free from any guilt that she might have felt had she not made the sacrifice. Our time together has not been marred by guilt and regret. Nevertheless, it was not easy for either of us to wait and use our time productively. Yet that was what we did. I rented an apartment in Columbia, moved some furniture from the country, and looked for ways to become meaningfully involved in my new home.

Angie and I had planned to retire, enjoy our rural surroundings, and perhaps look for some involvement in our new community, but those plans were no longer relevant. I was living alone in a city where I knew no one. I needed to set up a support system, arrange transportation, establish ways to shop for food and other necessities, and most of all, find activities that would prove to be interesting and rewarding. I was no longer young. I was blind, and I was not known. I did not want to seek employment, nor did I believe that meaningful employment was likely to be available had I sought it. Once again, I needed to create a life for myself, but now I lived at the intersection of aging and disability. I had the financial resources to support myself comfortably, but I could not be happy living alone, not having involvements, and not using my knowledge and experience to contribute to something outside myself. As always when I faced the need for a new direction, when I faced the need to create a new life, I read, wrote, and waited for inspiration.

During the summer I read a number of books that focused on American history, especially dealing with the US expansion into the Pacific region. I had always enjoyed reading American history, and I decided that I would like to seriously study our nation's origins. I contacted the history department at the University of Missouri and enrolled in two graduate courses for the fall semester. In the fall, I made application for the doctorial program and was accepted for degree studies. For the next four years, I lived the life of a graduate student while I waited for Angie.

It was an interesting time. I had no career goals attached to my studies. I already held a PhD degree. The students with whom I studied were closer to the age of my grandchildren than they were to mine, and the professors were the age of my daughter. Yet I enjoyed the work and benefited from the discipline required to study in a competitive advanced academic program.

The intellectual climate had changed in the thirty years since I studied at the University of Chicago. At that time, scholars looked for themes that gave unity to the American experience, but contemporary researchers pursue themes of diversity, the deconstruction of grand theories, and the experience of a broader range of the American people. Initially, this new atmosphere required some adjustment, but I had to acknowledge that I had lived the change. The work that I did as an advocate for persons with disabilities exemplified the change in American thought. Thirty years ago, no one gave a thought to persons with disabilities as a group worthy of having a serious history. However, a group of contemporary scholars are documenting the history of the oppression that the disabilities community has encountered and the admirable struggle that persons with disabilities have conducted for recognition, equality, and opportunity. The contemporary historians are presenting a much different vision of the American experience than previously has been the norm. Hypocrisy, oppression, conflict, and self-serving claims to exceptionalism are regular themes in the research of today's historical writers. I found this new historiography to be challenging and a little shocking, but in the end it rang true to my own experience.

I chose Francis Wayland, the evangelical Baptist Church leader and president of Brown University, for my dissertation research. Wayland was interesting to me because in the decades before the Civil War, he embodied the drift toward abolition that occurred among many northern religious leaders. He worked on a variety of reform movements, including public education, prison reform, and adult education. This group of moderate reformers hoped to overcome the evils of the social order and convert America to a Christian nation. They were optimistic and dedicated, but they could not prevent the war over slavery or the evolution of America into an imperial power, nor could they prevent the rise of the robber barons. Their optimism went underground as the forces of technology, economic development, and racism conquered nineteenth-century America.

Francis Wayland understood what was happening, but he lacked the power and the ideas to do anything about it. He died at the end of the Civil War, his dreams unrealized, his reputation marred, his way of life lost in the dynamics of a harsh new reality. The tragedy of America is that men like Francis Wayland ceased to be role models for our culture. But perhaps it is equally a tragedy that men like Wayland were not able to change enough with the times to bring a credible critical voice to the America that emerged after 1865. In Francis Wayland, I found a man who helped me understand the struggles of the liberal spirit in America to combat the forces of racism, exploitation of the American people and natural environment, and the growing harshness of the culture.

Even though my work at the university was engaging, it was not enough. I have always needed involvement in my community to be happy. In June 2005, I applied for a position on the Columbia Disabilities Commission and was appointed. In December, the commission members elected me the chairperson of the body, a position that I have held to the time of this writing. During this time, the commission has successfully promoted greater accessibility, inclusion of persons with disabilities in the civil rights protections guaranteed by the city, and the importance of an enhanced awareness of the disabilities community in all forms of city services and planning. My position with the commission has provided me with the opportunity to become involved with the politics of the city and to become acquainted with the workings of the community. This has been important to me, but my involvement with the Columbia Disabilities Commission has also opened other opportunities for engaging the community.

The mayor appointed me to a committee studying the need for increasing the stock of affordable housing in Columbia. This led to the creation of a nonprofit organization named Community Housing Options (CHO), which had as its purpose the development of accessible, affordable housing for persons with disabilities. I joined a community planning effort and worked with the project to build a long-range vision for the city. I joined the board of directors of Services for Independent Living, an independent living center serving persons with disabilities in a seven-county area in mid-Missouri, and chaired its board for three years. I was elected to the Central Committee of the Boone County Democratic Party and became its chairperson. As the years passed, I sunk roots in the Columbia community. My circle of friends grew. My involvements in community activities expanded, and my sense of happiness prospered in my new home. Angie joined me in 2009, and we were married. I felt intellectually and personally fulfilled, but in the midst of this new chapter of my life, a great challenge appeared that has dampened my joy of life in this last decade.

On June 2, 2006, I received a phone call from an investigator in the office of the Attorney General of Colorado. She said that she wanted to give me a heads-up warning. I, along with nine other persons, had been indicted by a grand jury under the Colorado Organized Crime Act. The allegations in the indictment claimed that I had conspired with the others to misdirect millions of dollars from bingo revenue to our personal use. The charges were serious felonies, and she advised me to get legal counsel. I was completely shocked by the allegations. I knew that I had not been involved in any such conspiracy nor had any of the others included in the indictment. I could not understand the motivation behind this action and I am still not completely sure what it was, but it soon became clear what was at stake.

The attorney general, John Suthers, was engaged in a reelection campaign. His media machine created a major event out of the indictment. A number of statewide newspapers and TV stations published accounts drawn from the AG's press release. The public relations office sold the indictment as the actions of the attorney general to protect the public from an organized criminal effort to take money from innocent victims. The AG's website carried a large account of the indictment on its first page. While I had committed no crime, the press listened only to the AG's office. My hard-earned reputation was severely damaged, and I was thrown into an almost two-year ordeal that was expensive and deeply embarrassing; it left me with a sense of violation that will never completely go away.

A grand jury meets behind closed doors. Those under investigation have no right to be represented during the proceedings. The prosecutor can present any information that he or she desires. The truth or relevance of that information cannot be challenged. A defendant can only have a part of the proceedings after an indictment is handed down. In my case, I received the testimony given during the deliberations of the grand jury, but I could not receive the instructions of the prosecutor from the AG's office. Later it was rumored within the AG's office that he had been promised that if he got an indictment from the grand jury, the attorney general would see that he received an appointment to a judgeship. A few months after the indictment was handed down, he was appointed to such a position. Nevertheless, the testimony demonstrated that the case was built on complete falsehoods; a misleading picture of the finances associated with the operation of the bingo enterprise, and unsupported hypothetical scenarios.

The crux of the allegations was that shell nonprofit organizations had been established that had no activities fulfilling the public purpose for which they were established. These organizations conducted bingo and used the money for the private use of the persons involved with the bingo enterprise. The indictment charged that a conspiracy to misuse bingo funds had yielded the participants up to $8,000,000 in ill-gotten gains. It made a juicy story in a world looking for sensational stories, but it was utterly untrue and laced with gross incompetence, or worse.

While the lead investigator for the AG's office was previously a staff person in the office that regulated the bingo industry, she demonstrated a total lack of knowledge of the bingo operation. Over 80 percent of revenue is immediately paid out in winnings to the players, rent to the hall where the games are played, and supplies used in the games. Yet this obvious reality was ignored in her investigation. She asserted that this money was missing and had been taken by those associated with the games. Her assertions came even though records, bank accounts, and filings with the Secretary of State's Office proved otherwise. Since the charges were dropped before the case went to court, there is no explanation for such assertions, but I can only wonder why she would make such obviously fallacious claims under oath. Was it incompetence or ambition, or was it instructions from higher authorities? I will never know, but the willingness to destroy the lives of others for personal gain, for whatever reason, is a deeply disturbing aspect of this whole affair.

Angie, her mother and father, and I were pressured to take plea bargains to settle the case, but we refused. Our cases dragged on for over two years before all the charges were finally dropped. I am not aware of a more blatant example of prosecutorial abuse, but it makes little difference. The newspaper articles remain on the Internet, and anyone can find them. Even though the charges were dropped and I had committed neither a legal nor a moral offense, the newspaper coverage of my vindication is brief and understated when compared with the sensationalism that surrounded the attorney general's announcement of the indictment. My public reputation has been marred, and there is little that I can do about it.

An anonymous person has given electronic copies of the newspaper articles to local organizations with which I am involved and threatened to go to the press with them if I receive an appointment to a leadership position within those organization. Even though this threat is empty, the texts of those articles raise doubt with anyone who does not know the facts in the episode. The outrage that I feel as the result of this injustice has challenged my equanimity and threatened to seriously cloud my joy of living in the last decades of my life. However, I refuse to grant this victory to the vicious predators that represented the office of the attorney general during this personally trying time.

As I age, I find that I need to consider new realities. I lack the physical strength or mental energy to take on the demanding commitments that filled my life in years gone by. I do not have the years to grow in an organization or position as I did in the past. I have less ability to discover the joy in life from doing, and increasingly I experience the happiness of living in less-challenging activities. In recent years, my friends and family have provided me with genuine pleasure. Angie and I have traveled extensively. I have continued to be active in my community, and I take pleasure in following the baseball Cardinals. I am finding ways to give of myself to others and engage the world around me. I feel useful to others and to my community, even though at a reduced level from that of the past. My health remains good, and I look forward to many years of happy living.

I am comfortable with my growing limitations, and I am not going to allow either the aging process or my blindness to prevent me from engaging realistically the larger world that I inhabit. A blind person must learn to live within the limitations of blindness, while at the same time she or he must refuse to accept artificial limitations. In the same way, the aging process imposes limitations, but there is no need to accept the premise that because I cannot do all that I once could, I cannot do anything. I will always push out the boundaries of my limitations in my efforts to engage my world. In this effort, I find my zest for life and my power to overcome disappointment and failure, discrimination and injustice, loss and heartbreak. It is my goal to live well for as long as I can, and then to die well, knowing that I tried very hard to make the world mine. No one can take this approach to life away from me.

Over the last several years, I have grown closer to my brother and sister and their families, and to my new family that Angie has shared with me. My daughter, son-in-law, and grandchildren continue to light up my life, and my relationship with my wife brings me great happiness. My extended family is a source of love and affection in the last decades of my life. My brother and I talk most every Sunday morning on the phone, recalling the events of our childhoods and adult lives, sharing our present lives, and reflecting on the wonders of living. My sister and I share our blindness and the challenges of leadership in the blind community. Angie has helped me to know her daughter, sister and brother-in-law, and nieces and nephews. My grandchildren are growing into successful young adults. Kelsie, my granddaughter, has cystic fibrosis, but she has not let this disease prevent her from claiming the larger world for her own. She is a college student and in 2011 was the lead dancer in a group known as the Silhouettes, which placed second in the national *America's Got Talent* television competition. We share our families and find that they bring us all the joys and frustrations of human bonding. We are enriched enormously by this wonderful group of relatives.

In May 2013, Angie and I and her father spent two weeks in Spain. She and I immensely enjoy travel. In the last several years, we have visited St. Martins in the Caribbean, Mexico, Italy, and Greece, and several locations in the United States. Our time in Spain was especially meaningful, because it gave us the opportunity to explore a rich historical and cultural part of the world where we had not been before. It allowed us to engage the world of the ancient Mediterranean and new Europe. We widened our horizons and deepened our understanding of our own roots in Western civilization, and above all, it allowed us to contemplate the joy inherent in being alive. The experience remains a high point of my life. It is difficult to capture such an intense experience in words, but in the following paragraphs, I offer my attempt to describe the joy of life that can be contained in such an experience.

Angie and I stood in the wet sand, where just a few hours ago the tide covered the beach, and listened to the waves wrap around the rocks to our right that extended into the sea. Listening carefully, the roar of the sea became not just one sound, but an orchestra with many instruments playing their separate parts. There was the slap of the waves as they hit the sand, the shorter sounds of the waves after they broke on the rocks, and longer, more powerful sounds from those waves farther out. Within each wave were smaller sounds: spray hitting the water, the wave rolling along the surface as it came toward us, and amid all the sounds, a sense of a driving force that was beyond our power to affect.

The sound of the sea feels infinite, outside of time. It creates a fear and awe. Standing before the mindless roar of the sea, we felt the limits of our short lives. There was also a feeling that we shared the importance of this moment together. In this moment, we recognized that duality of human existence. We stood against the overwhelming power of the natural order, and we stood within that order, the children of its creation. It was comforting and powerfully harmonizing to know that we live together in the fear and awe of time and space along the sea. We know that it will thunder on after we are gone. In this moment, though, it was ours to contemplate. It opened us to a deeper and more profound grasp of our place in all the cosmos. We are small and vulnerable, yet connected to all that is. Our support for one another and sharing overcomes our isolation and dread. The moment was magic.

Angie said, "It is beautiful out here."

I ask her, "What does beautiful mean?"

She thought and then answered my question. "The sun has disappeared, but there are still dark blues and purples in the sky. The water reflects the colors of the sky, and far out the sea and the sky merge. I can see the lights along the shore. It feels so peaceful."

In my imagination, I pictured what she was saying, and the image that I envisioned was, indeed, beautiful.

Angie, her father, and I traveled in Spain for two weeks. We spent our first week on the Costa del Sol near Malaga in the province of Andalusia. We stayed in a resort called Leila Playa. I am blind, and my wife is sighted. We are experienced travelers. I often write about our travels, and she captures them with her photographs. We are partners, sharing our experiences, enriching our travel and our lives as we share our knowledge, sight, and insight.

So much of the joy of travel is visual. A traveler is a stranger to the landscape, the human-built environment, and the people. The spoken language is frequently unknown. The first entry into this new world is through visual observation. The traveler stands apart and views the new surroundings, looking for recognizable patterns, making judgments, gathering impressions that form an understanding of the new world. A blind traveler must gather visual information from another person, or compensate for not having it with careful listening and strategic use of his or her other senses. This takes time, and the traveler seldom stays long enough at any single place to absorb what the spot has to offer, so sharing the experience with a sighted companion can be extremely helpful.

As a blind traveler, I must engage the visit actively. I must ask questions that force my companion to see more clearly. We must study details together. As a blind person, I build an image of the new environment; my companion also deepens her visual image. Only partners who care for one another and have the patience to share the experience can make this process of looking and learning work. Angie and I have learned the art of sharing, and as we enrich our understanding of the new world that we are entering, we experience the joy of discovery that makes travel so much a part of human happiness.

We landed at the Malaga airport a few hours earlier. When we walk together, I take Angie's hand or arm. We have learned to travel quickly and with coordination through crowded areas. I load our carry-on bags on my shoulders, hold my white cane in my right hand, and take Angie's hand. Attuned to her movement, we dance through the throngs of our fellow passengers. We pass through passport control and customs. Angie takes the passports out of my front pocket, where she keeps them for rapid retrieval, and shows them to the officials. After they wave us through, we claim our bags. While Angie goes to the rental car desk, I guard our luggage. As we go to our car, I carry and pull our bags, but Angie has luggage also. I maintain contact with her bag with my cane, and I follow her voice through the congested terminal. In a few minutes, our car is packed, and we are on the road headed to our resort.

Angie found the correct route with only moderate difficulty. As soon as she was settled in, I asked, "What do you see?"

She said, "It looks very clean. The roadside is covered with flowers and landscaping. The trees are blooming. It looks very deliberately cared for. Off to our left, you can see the Mediterranean. It is beautiful. The water is a tapestry of many shades of blue. Off in the distance to the right, you can see mountains. They are very green."

Angie easily found our resort, and we moved into our apartment. It was modern and well equipped. I explored its arrangement, so that I could move comfortably around and serve myself in the kitchen. In a little while, we were ready to explore the grounds. The beach and sea were a few yards from our front door, but first we chose to walk through the gardens. Built on a hill, the resort rises up from the beach. She and I ascended a path through a series of terraced gardens that led up to the central office at the entrance to the property. We walked up the path, stopping to examine the flowers and shrubs. Angie placed my hands on the blossoms, and I felt their rich, glossy texture. I bent over to take in their fragrance. I ran my hand along the smoothly trimmed shrubbery and recognized the talent and work that had gone into the maintenance of these gardens. We listened to the roar of the sea and absorbed the blend of nature and human cultivation that made this place a satisfying refuge.

After a night's rest, we were ready to explore our environment. All of the travel commentaries report that overdevelopment of tourist hotels and resorts have ruined the west end of the Costa del Sol, the area where we were staying. So we were curious to find if we agreed. Our resort had about thirty units. They were low-rise and very attractive, with the units surrounding the central gardens, waterfalls, and ponds. The gardens and beach are well cared for. We had no sense of being crowded, but we did see many high-rise condominiums on our drive from the airport. They blocked the view of the sea, and Angie and her father agreed that they mar the beauty of the water and the mountains. We have heard that many of these sites are in disrepair, but we were never able to confirm that as fact.

We began our exploration of the area in Fuengirola, a small town about twenty kilometers to the east, toward Malaga. We were drawn to a promenade that ran along the sea, lined with restaurants and shops. A marina harbored some impressive private crafts, and an entertainment center that extended into the harbor featured live music. It seemed to be a typical tourist location, although there were younger people just hanging out who seemed to be local teenagers. We read advertisements in real estate office windows for houses and apartments for sale and rent. These notices confirmed that the Spanish housing market was experiencing some of the turmoil that plagued the American market a few years earlier. Fuengirola seemed pleasant enough to us, but rather mediocre. Then we found something that was not ordinary.

A man accosted us in a combination of Spanish and English. "You must come," he said. "I will serve you fresh fish. I will fillet it at your table."

We were not certain, but after some conversation with him, Angie, who speaks some Spanish, gave us an okay, and we went into his establishment. We sat in an open, large, barnlike structure, with large picture windows all the way around, very near the sea. A strong breeze drove us inside, although more-hardy souls sat outside on a patio. This was where Angie wanted to sit, but she was outnumbered two to one.

Our host highly recommended the fresh fish. He said that after grilling it over a fire on the beach, he would bring it to our table and fillet it for us. We chose a Mahi Mahi fresh from the sea. While we waited for our main course, we were served an appetizer of sardines, marinated in herbs and spices with olive oil, tomatoes, and Spanish olives. We ordered wine, and in due time, the man returned with our fish. The fish still had its head and fins, but it was done and the outside was crispy. He took a fork and spoon and removed the skin, and then he began carving the meat from the bones and filled our plates. He served our fish with potatoes, a salad, and Spanish rolls.

As we sipped our wine, enjoyed the best seafood we had ever eaten, felt the breeze blow over us, and smelled the salt sea and fish aroma, we recognized that this would be a moment that we would not forget. It was a moment of enjoyment and closeness to the goodness of life that we would always remember sharing. It was truly one of those great moments of living. One does not need vision to absorb the power of the sea, the history of the ancient site, the excellence of the meal, and the warmth of a loving family. These ecstatic joys exist in the heart, mind, and soul of the beholder. They connect us to the land and the sea, the history and the culture, and the soul of Spain. They are enchanted moments. They are among the richest of the rewards that come to those who learn to recognize them. They are independent of sight. They belong to the realm of insight and imagination. While the boom and bust of the Spanish tourism industry has marred the beauty of the Costa del Sol, much remains for those who have not lost the power of a simple heart to look for meaning in a complex land.

I am now living in the eighth decade of my life. As I reflect on the past, I realize the many mistakes that I made and the many paths that I did not take that might have been more interesting or productive or brought me greater happiness. Yet I continue to believe that life must be lived forward. I take pleasure in recalling my past, but my happiness lies in what I can make of the future. In whatever time is left in my life, I hope to use the resources that I have to squeeze out every ounce of enchantment that I can from every moment that I have. I am blind, I am aging, I have limitations, but I am still in the game, and I intend to play it until the end.

In the years ahead, I plan to assist persons with disabilities to tell their stories. Angie and I will travel and enjoy our family and friends, and I will write. We will engage our community and reach out to those who may need our assistance. I will not chase thrills to prove that I am still alive. I will not jump out of an airplane on my eightieth birthday or climb a mountain, but I will cherish the everyday pleasures and challenges.

Once a friend asked me to sum up my philosophy in a single word. My one-word answer was "affirmation." Affirmation does not mean naive optimism. It embraces a mature understanding that living often holds pain and suffering, injustice and betrayal, and irrational and meaningless violence and destruction. It is the courage to affirm life in the face of the challenge of meaninglessness, despair, and death. It is the stubborn insistence that generosity and tolerance are values that make life dear, even though there are others who attempt to impose their own patterns of value on a world that they fear. I affirm this life as all that there is. It is neither a test for some other existence, nor an every-man-for-himself struggle for success in a valueless war for survival and dominance. Human happiness is a continuing affirmation of the wonder of life amid the forces of cynicism and fanaticism, natural disaster and human folly, misunderstood complexity and the impersonality of a gigantic, incomprehensible universe. Yet the joy of living fills the being of each person who experiences it with value that is beyond any other treasure that human experience can create. I know and affirm this joy of living. It is my story. I live in the intersection of aging and disability. It is a location where I feel at home and discover the peace that flows from a life that I can affirm.